AF656427

~~HIRED~~

~~FIRED~~

# TIRED.

# ~~HIRED~~ ~~FIRED~~ TIRED.

*A Brown Woman's Manual To Thrive In Tech*

TUSHARA REDDY

NU VOICE PRESS

First published by NU VOICE PRESS 2026
An imprint of Hubhawks Pvt. Ltd
www.nuvoicepress.com



This is a work of non-fiction. Space and time have been rearranged to suit the convenience of the book. Except for public figures, hotels, and institution names, any resemblance to persons living or dead or the real events are purely coincidental. The opinions expressed in the book are those of the characters, and should not be confused with that of the Author.



ISBN: 978-81-996780-6-4
Typeset in Goudy Old Style 11.5 pt
Published by Nu Voice Press
Printed at Manipal Technologies Limited, Manipal

Dedicated to the millions of Indian talents behind the black screen, toiling into the wee hours of the day. Seldom noticed, thanked, or recognised for their genius.

# Contents

# Prologue: The Spiral

I stood at the Tower Bridge wondering—if I jumped, would they convict me for attempted suicide? Or if I died, would I finally be liberated from this relentless yap of a life?

I didn't hit rock bottom; I found myself a thousand feet below the ocean bed, metaphorically. As I imagined that free fall into the Thames, my whole life flashed before me like a sixty-second Instagram reel: my birth, my first pet, my first love, the first time my parents beat the crap out of me, my first salary, my first betrayal, my first tryst with the devil himself. Everything passed in a storm of energy, purging me of the karma of this lifetime.

My skin touched the cold London waters, in imagination or spirit, I can't quite tell, as I plunged into the depths of the Thames. The splash drew startled faces on the bridge above. Traffic slowed; people leaned over the rails. Uber boats and yachts sliced through the current while water rushed into my drowning lungs, and I simply... allowed it.

It was in that moment, when I almost left the mortal plane behind, that I began spiralling through a tunnel. Inside it were snippets of **all** possible versions of my life. The same souls, the same circumstances, but in infinite combinations: love, hate, betrayal, lust, kindness, greed, redemption. I saw them all through their eyes and their auras, embodied in different lives, performing the same karmic dance in new costumes.

I realised that every crossroad of life leads to the same dark spiral. We go in circles, eternally entangled in vibration. There was no white light at the end of the tunnel, no godly hand. I saw my darkest despairs, my most luminous highs—sunrise at

Monument Valley, the last kiss I shared with my beloved—and I understood: death is not the answer.

We rush through life with such false urgency, as if our worth could be measured by a wristwatch. But time in this mortal plane has nothing to do with clocks. We are entities with innate vibrations, spinning with a specific quark of purpose until the matrix, the maya, calls us back.

When we enter this reality, we choose a mission. The rest: the drama, the thoughts, the desires, the disappointments, are tricks of the mind. We are essentially on autopilot, spinning through permutations until we either evolve beyond the spiral or return again—as a shark, a bug, a tree, a laptop, or a flea—each form fulfilling a fragment of that mission. If you're lucky, you escape the spiral; if not, you re-enter it, slap-resurrected into another cycle.

So, what's the way out, upward or downward? And does direction even matter? Perhaps not. The purpose is to go through life—to suffer, to rejoice, to feel the rawest emotions human consciousness can bear. To experience love in all its divine, lustful, immobilising glory. To question, to hate, to surrender, and in that surrender, to realise your only purpose is to keep moving through the spiral, or die trying.

And then I woke up to the shrieking alarm.

I checked my phone and found an ad hoc one-on-one with my manager.

The past couple of months had been such a tussle with him. During these sessions, I was already expecting the worst.

The problem with being an immigrant employee is that losing your job doesn't just mean losing your paycheck; it means losing your entire existence.

It's not just a job. It's your visa, your home, your right to stay, your fragile illusion of belonging.

It's your years of effort relocating, the student loan still haunting you, the dream of building a life in a city that both loves and rejects you—all hanging by the thread of a sponsorship letter.

And he knew that.

He was using that classic British tactic: polite psychological warfare. Slowly crawling into my head in such a subtle way that I'd start over-reflecting and second-guessing myself every time he gave "constructive" feedback.

Still, I had no choice but to walk in—like Abhimanyu walking into the *Chakravyuha*, knowing he only knew how to enter but not how to get out.

Such is the story of many immigrants working in tech, stepping into this capitalist maze that pays the bills but quietly steals your spirit.

You wake up one morning and realise you've traded your native sky for a sponsored cubicle.

You survive in PowerPoint slides and Jira tickets, while your family calls from 5,000 miles away asking when you're getting married.

You start talking in acronyms: ROI, KPI, MVP, as if success is a formula that can keep your soul from collapsing.

Why does a vast majority of Indian youth still aspire to work in the private sector? Because there isn't much else left.

Reservation quotas, bribes for government jobs, startup ecosystems that glorify founders but starve them of funds, and agricultural lives that break backs but not cycles.

So, we march into the Chakravyuha—laptops as shields, KPIs as arrows, burnout as destiny—hoping to somehow break through.

And in that instant, standing in front of my screen, I made a quiet promise to myself:

If I ever came out of this spiral alive, I would speak my truth, raw and unapologetic.

For every immigrant who built a dream on borrowed time and every woman who was told her ambition was arrogance.

For every son too scared to tell his parents he's depressed because he's "made it abroad." For every daughter who stayed up all night refreshing her visa status.

For every brown, brilliant, burnt-out professional who wanted more out of life than deliverables and dependency.

A word to the reader: the Immigrant, the Outsider, and the Restless Dreamer.

Hey, you—the relentlessly talented one second-guessing yourself—have the confidence of your average male colleague who markets himself like Ogilvy while the only productive thing he does all day is breathe.

I know you're juggling work, deadlines, rent, paperwork, maybe relationships, maybe parents on another continent.

You're surviving feedback loops, imposter syndrome, appraisals, rejections, and the cold indifference of systems designed to use you, not grow you.

And you're wondering, what's wrong with me?

Through this book, let me help you the way I helped myself.

I'm not a psychologist. I'm not employee-of-the-year. I don't even work at one of the FAANG firms.

So, what qualifies me to speak? Nothing—except that I've lived through my own personal hell, and walked back with my sanity, scars, and spirit intact.

And on my way back, I became sensitive to the quiet pain people carry: in accents, in resumes, in immigration files, in silences.

Before we begin this journey through LED screens, code consoles, complete assholes, work dogs and office politics, why don't you write down your deepest insecurity with respect to work:

- I don't know enough about AI to lead an AI team, although I have a MSc in AI.
- My startup is too small to matter, although it is providing employment to 100s.
- I'm a temporary resource in a permanent system, although I am exceptionally efficient at my job.
- My Indian accent gives me away before my work does.
- I'm replaceable.

**And then write down your most audacious goal:**

- To build a unicorn that would address the waste management problem in India.
- I will ask out Bradley Cooper, even if there is finite risk of rejection.
- To build ethical AI products that solves an actual problem not just burn VC money.

- To prove that kindness precedes niceness.
- To be the immigrant who doesn't just survive abroad, but thrives–visibly, unapologetically.

By the end of this book, we'll revisit both lists and you'll see how your darkest side is not your downfall, but your vault.

The locked door that, when opened, leads straight to your best life.

Because it's only by walking through your demons that you meet your divine.

Use this format:

**I, (your name), want to (build / become / overcome / evolve out of) __________ for (reason / purpose) __________ by (tentative deadline).**

P.S. A goal without a deadline is merely a wish. A deadline without purpose is just another task. Write it down. Let it exist outside your head. Let it hold you accountable as you move through my journey–perhaps recognising fragments of your own. Empathising. Learning. And, if you allow it, healing.

# Chapter 1: WTF is Happening Inside the Tech World?

Before we make sense of what is changing so rapidly, let's align on one simple question.

**What Do We Actually Mean by the "Tech World"?**

In this book, the tech world refers to the IT services industry [17], the invisible machinery that powers almost every modern business. If it involves computers, software, data, networks, or the internet, it likely falls under IT services.

At its core, IT services include:

- Helping businesses decide what technology they need and why (consulting)
- Building software, applications, and websites (development)
- Making different systems work together seamlessly (integration)
- Hosting infrastructure on servers or cloud platforms
- Keeping systems secure, stable, and continuously running (support and maintenance)

We're talking about an industry whose global market share is valued at **$1.54 trillion as of 2025 [1],** and India is one of its largest exporters of human capital. Consulting, software development, IT-enabled services... you name it, we send it. Nearly **5.4 million** [2] people in the Indian subcontinent alone are grinding away in tech, contributing a full **7% of the country's GDP [3] [15].** We are one of the largest IT talent exporters globally. IT and BPO services comprise over 60% of India's service exports [21], yet nobody gives a tiny rat's ass about the actual lives, health, or mental stability of these "geeky" geniuses that the world depends on.

### Geopolitical Factors

Now that we have seen the umpteen opportunities of the IT industry, let's delve into the problems, both macro and micro level, from the perspective of employees. Let me spell it out: software professionals face some of the highest risks for heart disease and stroke–long hours, brutal hire-and-fire norms, geopolitical nonsense (thank you, President of the USA), three years of explosive AI evolution, global layoffs, and the new corporate fashion trend of "lean teams" where **one person now does the job of three**. But who exactly is safeguarding these workers?

Spoiler: **no one.**

The insecurity is relentless:

- job instability
- unclear future for their roles
- companies collapsing overnight
- the complete myth of "work-life balance"

### Challenges While Working or Studying Abroad

Don't even get me started on visa-sponsored jobs abroad. In the glamorous West, the global *desi* is both a threat and a cash cow. Patterns are painfully obvious: random mass layoffs targeting immigrants, bonded-labour expectations from visa-dependent employees, and Global Capability Centres (GCCs) acting as nothing but the administrative back offices for the Bay Area.

When I moved to the UK—to pursue my post-graduation at a Russell Group university, funded by an Indian education loan—I landed in one of the world's most expensive cities: London. From the end of 2021 to early 2025, I woke up with the same nightmare: cost of living crisis, fear of being replaced by someone offshore or inability to secure UK work **visa sponsorship [5].** One wrong org restructuring (refer to Glossary) , one unexpected market downturn, and your entire life collapses like a house of cards.

Why did I take such a massive, uncalculated risk? Because like millions of young Indians, I believed the foreign-passport dream: better lifestyle, no nosy relatives, stable infrastructure, safer public spaces. And yes, some of that came true: transport, weather, working hours, team culture—brilliant! But abroad comes with its own demons. Visa quotas are tight, sponsorship slots are reserved for unicorn employees, and the 18–24-month Post-Study Work Visa (Graduate Visa) in the UK (36 months in the US) becomes a **countdown timer to panic [5].**

## Burdensome Student Loans

Student loans? They range from ₹2 million – ₹20 million depending on your course, university brand, and the ROI your parents fantasise about. In my case, I got hired by a UK-based MNC. I was a star performer—until sponsorship time arrived and they dropped the "strategic restructuring" excuse.

So two years of **"I will prove my worth"** went straight to the dogs because some dude in California decided to merge two organisations and dissolve ours.

Just like that, my London dream folded. My only choice was to drag myself back to the Silicon sweatshop we lovingly call Bengaluru—the global tech back office—and figure out how to repay my student loan while trying to revive my career.

## Why are Indians Obsessed with the Tech World?

As a **first-generation tech professional**, you are the most vulnerable creature in this entire ecosystem. Every weak spot, financial, emotional, social, is fully exposed. And being a young, good-looking woman in this industry? That adds ten more layers of risk. The majority will pretend otherwise, but the tech world can be just as predatory as Bollywood's casting couches—the only difference is the lighting.

You might wonder, "If this industry is so full of thorns, why enter it at all?"

Simple: **we have no other choice.**

In India, competing for government jobs is like signing up for a lifetime of misery. Medicine, law, liberal arts, all have insane demand-supply gaps. Engineering becomes the cheapest, most predictable escape route. Companies scoop freshers straight out of their final semester, peel them off wooden benches, and stick them onto ergonomic chairs.

Entry-level salaries? Stagnant at **₹300,000–₹800,000** for a decade.

Many graduates, both in India and abroad, continue working as cashiers, bartenders, tutors, and baristas even after completing their degrees just to remain financially afloat while searching for jobs that actually match their skill sets.

## Struggles of Finding Employment – Abroad or Inland

Recruitment isn't innocent either. ATS systems are outdated relics that need code exorcisms. With advanced summarisation models available, we're still failing to match talent with jobs. Networking helps until it doesn't, often turning into a cesspool where people in power ask for **sexual favours** in exchange for interview referrals. The #MeToo movement didn't even scratch the corporate surface. That world is darker.

Now with generative AI, applicants are morphing job descriptions into resumes with ChatGPT. Recruiters struggle between evaluating skills and calculating visa risks. Your pedigree might get you shortlisted, but your marital status, skin colour, age, reproductive timeline, and willingness to be a corporate work-dog determines whether you get the offer.

**Gender Disparity**

All those "Women in Tech" initiatives?

Corporate greenwashing, just like petroleum companies pretending to care about the climate.

This industry doesn't want diversity. It wants **obedient labour**.

Any amount of spine, clarity, or courage must be locked away before entering the building.

And here's where mythology hits the nerve:

Karna, in the *Mahabharata*, wanted to escape his inherited identity. Born to charioteer lineage, he aspired to be a warrior, a ruler, a kingmaker. But society punished him for daring to rise above his caste station.

**First-generation Indian tech professionals** are modern-day Karna's.

Our parents came from farming, real estate, tailoring, dairy, microfinance, small businesses, honest work, but far from this industry. We are the first ones stepping into IT. And like Karna, we pay the price for daring to challenge our generational status quo.

Because after the colonial loot left India gasping for survival, the Green Revolution (1960s) revived agriculture, the White Revolution (1970s) boosted dairy, and finally the Digital Revolution (1980s onwards, powered by Infosys, TCS, Wipro) gave India a new identity: **the world's largest technological talent and services exporter [4].**

We became the **backbone of global tech—but at what cost?**

No one prepared us for this battlefield.

No one warned us about burnout, geopolitics, layoffs, visas, racial bias, gender bias, or predatory hiring.

No one told us the world's largest tech headcount is built on the bruised bodies and broken dreams of millions of Indians holding this industry together.

And that's the truth behind the trillion-dollar façade.

## Lagging in Authentic Tech Innovation

Indian techies deliver some of the highest-quality outputs in technical and engineering services. They are not only fluent in coding languages but are also fluent in the English language. This deadly combination gives us ample competitive edge over thriving economies like China, the USA, the UK, and Japan.

The flexibility, strong work ethic, and personal stability exhibited by Indian professionals are among the highest across cultures, making them a great catch for critical roles.

*Why are we still lagging behind in real tech innovations, not "potayto-potahto" startups?*

**For starters:** Unfair working hours, inadequate compensation, limited access to mental health professionals who understand the nuances of tech-specific pressures, restricted opportunities for individual growth, a lack of transparency in top-down decision-making, and unclear career pathways—exacerbated by the fear of being replaced by AI—are evident and persistent!

**One simply cannot innovate in survival mode. Innovation requires some level of psychological security, apart from financial, emotional, and physical well-being, of course!**

How can organisations, governments, and individuals ensure this at a practical level—not just passing labour policy reforms in the Indian Lower House, such as proposed limits on working hours to 12 hours a day, or by spreading awareness about mental health in the workplace? How can one really implement such norms to see tangible changes in the everyday lives and well-being of employees?

# Chapter 2: My Manager is Toxic; Should I Quit My Job?

I hear a fair share of corporate employees crib about having a troubled working relationship with their immediate manager. As someone who has been on both sides of the table, I have even seen managers crib about shoddy team members, because of whom they dread Mondays. Well, if we remove these designations, we are all just people—at worst, monkeys with some skills. Each thumping the face of the earth, presuming his skill is more crucial than the other one's. What we truly need is a little bit of perspective. Remember you applied for that job, prayed, wished, and begged the universe to give it to you. So, you having an issue at your work is actually the universe working in your favour. So, if you act ungratefully, then the universe feels unrewarded.

**Struggle with Authoritative Relationships**

I know you must be thinking that I have this temperamental, pain-in-the-ass manager whom I need to face tomorrow in the weekly one-to-one—what is this author preaching about? Well, as a human being, you must work in some sort of hierarchy. Even if you decide to start up, you still have the hierarchy of board members, investors, banks, customers, mentors and what not. If you come from some money and decide to go passive income by building a bunch of houses and renting them out for a living, you still have tenant problems, dealing with maintenance folks and so on. So, the bottom line is no matter what you try to do in life, people are the potential, people are the problem. Some of the best experiences I have had in life are because of people and some of the worst hair-losing, thyroid-aggravating experiences have also been because of them.

## Avoid Temptation of Demonising!

First of all, if you have a dreadful relationship with your manager or subordinate or any team member, don't talk about it to anyone in office. I repeat, nobody means well. They will form perceptions about it in their head, they will weaponise it against you. You need to find ex-colleagues, mentors, or specific people who can provide sensible advice for a problem. If you just want to rant and get the frustration out of your system, you hire a shrink by the hour. Don't rant about office problems to your friends no matter how close you are, because it's not about you ranting to them: it's about the kind of advice they might give without having a complete context of the situation, which will blow the problem out of proportion. Trust me, everyone is going through shit. Their shit gives them shitty thoughts; when you add your shit on top of it, it doles out more shitty words in the form of advice, which you will take seriously because your ego has antagonised your colleague or manager and made your friend give advice that glorifies that aspect.

## Put Your Ego to Sleep, Function from Authenticity

In all honesty, deep down, we all know why certain problems exist, how much contribution we have made to that situation, and how to wriggle out of it. The problem is that our ego won't let us resolve it, because we have a narrative and want it to have an ending that makes us the hero of the story. But so does the other guy; he has to win his narrative too. So ideally, if this approach continues, you will only make enemies and burn bridges, making life hard for yourself. Because the global IT industry is very closely knit, as vast and spread across as it may sound, everyone is either using a product, working in its GCC, their service implementation or is their end-user or vendor. So, it's a domino effect. If one relationship goes bad, almost always either that frustration spreads to other relationships or the gossip spreads. You can always redeem yourself with great productivity and throughput, but the initial barrier would be higher than for others. Because you are beginning your professional relationship from a point of disadvantage. I would say always choose firm diplomacy. Be the most firm and authentic fucker around. But be very professional and authentic about it.

**Anecdote on Imbalanced Power Dynamics at Work**

Let me quote an example from my own career, when I was working with a London-based telecom company a couple of years ago. My then manager started making unnecessary advances towards me. The best part is I recognised it.

Let me explain this London-based telecom company's culture to anyone who has never experienced it (and I wish nobody ever does). I completed my MSc in Data Science, wrapped up my internship, and started making applications immediately. It was one December night in London, around 10 p.m., when I was lounging in my student dorm after dinner, that I received a call from a recruiter. They claimed to be working for this London-based telecom company, that my job application had been processed and that I was to interview the next day. I was dealing with my broken engagement, messed-up relationship with my parents, and understanding how wound up patriarchal society is (that is a story for another time). I was also running low on savings amidst the cost of living crisis in the UK and was too proud to ask my parents for any money. I ended up taking the first offer I got; I didn't ask around. In fact, I just saw the company profile online and took the job. Glassdoor, Owler or any other website never had anything shady about them. However, even as I walked into their facility I could sense something was off, but I ignored it as nervousness. I mean, it was one of the largest properties on the commercial district in the heart of Central London. The math added up to the company being financially stable and that I would get a visa sponsorship.

**Inappropriate Questions During Interviews**

I walked in for the interview, only to learn that my interviewer—who would later become my manager—was unavailable. Instead, I was asked to meet a member of the C-suite. He got straight to the point and asked why I needed the job. I gave what I believed was the most appropriate, technically sound response: that I aspired to work as a Global Product Manager for one of the leading telecom networks in the UK.

But his interest wasn't in my ambition or qualifications. He seemed more focused on how badly I needed the job—almost as if he were measuring my desperation rather than my capability. The conversation then took a disturbing turn. He asked whether I was married, and more pointedly, why I wasn't married yet.

At the time, I didn't fully grasp what was happening. It was only later that I began to understand how deeply toxic the hiring culture was. The organisation had a clear, unspoken preference: they hired conventionally attractive women, typically below the age of 30 or 35, often placing them on the same floor. Among the women themselves, this was discussed almost with pride—as if being hired was validation of their appearance rather than their competence.

About a month into the role, I found myself baffled by these revelations. For women in their late twenties to mid-thirties, interviews placed a disproportionate emphasis on marital status, childbearing, and familial responsibilities—

especially at a stage when roles become more serious and decision-making authority increases. Women who chose, or even hinted at wanting to balance professional ambition with personal life, were quietly sidelined, replaced, or overpowered.

This, unfortunately, remains a harsh and unspoken reality of hiring practices in the tech industry.

**Poor Company Culture**

There were Friday evening parties on the shop floor in the pantry where booze was served. It was compulsory to stay and attend because this was during the login hours and the company had strict policies that one had to login by 9 a.m. and logout by 6 p.m. only. I was terribly traumatised by the **sexism** in these parties, on top of which I had real work to get done in terms of analysing the fraudulent payments occurring on our online enrolment channels for the prepaid business. I mean, as a newly-graduated data science student to be solving a real-world problem was simply exciting for me. I was talking to legal about the various telecom compliance laws across the globe (Netherlands, Germany, UK, USA, Sweden, Australia) and to the on-field sale/product manager on how the local retail store owners were onboarding customers. I also had to work closely with the payment gateway implementation team to get the daily transaction data on how many transactions were failing from which payment gateway, and vendor screening new compliance software and debating their pros and cons to ensure there were no lawsuits slapped on our company. This was not an easy task because I was primarily telling the company how its revenue is leaking due to a bunch of softwares and people are outdated. Many people on the field disliked my audacity and conviction, because I am the get-it-done girl. I have always received some very odd problem statements all through my career which I have had the greatest pleasure of breaking down into simple iterative actionables and delegate them, monitor, and repeat.

In most of these cases, I didn't even know what the plan would be like in the next week or month, but I always knew what little effort it would require to know that unknown. Although I felt it was obviously my job to get going, I didn't realise politics would play a huge role. And that these compliance issues would land the company in serious lawsuits across France and other countries where they would hire a white CEO just to have his head hung. I didn't know my innocent root cause analysis was opening a Pandora's box that would internally expose moles who wanted this company to be sued, and I was, in some sense, saving them.

**Sexual Advances at Workplace**

I was ranting about how inappropriate some of the comments on the floor were towards me, about my dressing or my skirt length and how I had to keep my eyes down as I worked. And I started revealing to my coworkers how some of my managers, in one-on-one interactions, were not professional, verbally and emotionally. He was either oversharing his marital problems or asking me to accompany him to a meeting with one of our vendors after office hours, which was really a late-night dinner he tricked me into. When I sensed this was taking the wrong direction, as he leaned in to *try to* kiss me in one of the one-on-one meetings in the office, I politely reminded him that he is married, he is my boss, and this is inappropriate.

Our working relationship got strained and he refused to approve my leave to visit India. He would downplay my work and even throw me under the bus at every opportunity he got. I was feeling a bit threatened, and it was distasteful. He would even call me post office hours to check where I was, or to invite himself over to dinner. To all of which I gave very clear responses such as, "I believe I could invite your wife and you for a dinner sometime, to get acquainted with you both." Besides this I had enrolled in a premium gym, which the office was paying for. Apparently, he "accidentally" bumped into me a couple of times. So, there was stalking, inappropriate advances at the workplace, and violation of personal space and boundaries. Why didn't I just go to HR? Because I once tried telling my manager I would do that and he said, quote: "HR is in the pockets of senior leadership, and I am senior leadership in this organisation." He further continued to offer me an apartment, divorce his company stake-holding millionaire wife, and move in with me if I decided to go ahead with his indecent proposal. To which I politely but under-confidently reacted as if it was a word play. I should have known he was a psychotic, ego-driven man who would make my life hell if I didn't stand up to him at the right time.

**Each to Their Own Mindset**

I sought help from the only senior female leader on the board. I thought perhaps seeking her intervention would help both comfort me from a female standpoint and maybe indirectly give me some hint to correct his ways. But that was one of the worst things I could have done. She first gaslit me into thinking women in the workplace need to deal with this, that rejecting a man's advances was inappropriate, especially on the grounds of age and marital status, and guilt-tripped me into a manipulated state of mind. I almost forgot whom I was up against. He was, after all, part of the senior leadership of one of the leading telecom companies in the UK, which at that point funded the UK's Conservative Party, which was in power. I was told that sleeping with him would not be a big deal morally and women should oblige when men in power demand sex in return for whatever is on the table. To which my enraged response was, "What, exactly, could he offer me that I do not already have—or cannot achieve through my own abilities?" Financial security? I am an educated woman, fully capable of supporting myself. Social status? I am an Indian woman, born and raised by respectable parents, from a long lineage of well-regarded scholars and landowners. How would being the girlfriend—or worse, a kept secret—of a married Sri Lankan man elevate my standing in any way?

Visa sponsorship? I could pursue another role or apply independently for a post-study work visa.

And as for intimacy or companionship, he was not even remotely aligned with what I value in a man—loyalty, decency, and self-respect.

**Price of Saying "No"**

Honestly, this response led to a domino effect when I took time off to visit my parents back home, after fighting for it with this tedious, ego-bruised man. At that moment, I remember feeling angry at the senior woman's advice, at the way she explained how society expects a woman to behave, and at fate itself for bringing me to these crossroads. I felt cornered and helpless; I even started to empathise with the perpetrator's state of mind, which is the worst kind of manipulation. But when I went back to India, which I felt was the best way to regain my lost self-confidence, I realised my values were what defined me. I was feeling enraged not because of what was happening to me, but because it was my inner consciousness or soul telling me this situation, these statements, or these people were not in alignment with my innate self. And the rage was more self-directed, as I was infuriated with the side of me which was trying to empathise with the perpetrator and trying to resolve the situation when it was a simple case of walking out. Remember, at this point my personal relationship with my parents was strained because I walked out on the "prized" trophy fiancé they had selected for me, who was a narcissist of the first order with psychotic anger issues. I was being gaslit for not being the calming presence in his life and all that. And in my moment of weakness, when I did reach out to them, they ended up asking if I did something to instigate this behaviour from that man. Well, at that point it further enraged me, but now that I think about it, they were all systematically brainwashed into thinking women are the problem in any situation. Even if it was your own blood, as opposed to absolute strangers, the gender was at fault, something absolutely out of my control or choice.

I asked my parents how they could question their own blood, their upbringing, a piece of their own flesh with this question, and they promptly responded, "Because you seem to always have problems. Why aren't your sister or other girls working abroad facing these issues? You also rejected the gorgeous looking prince of a man and made the poor guy shed a tear for you. There is a good chance you are the problem." My response to this was: "Hell no, you all are the problem! Sri Lanka, India—all these countries are South Asian with the same post-colonial conditioning that women plague society. They are fit for three and only three purposes—one to procreate. Two, to raise children, the man of the family being the biggest. Three to cook—food, stories, and problems."

So yes, I was up against a system which was rigid, timeless, and in the majority. I had my ex-colleague, turned friend, turned family, and his wife, who stood by me in those times and reminded me of my true potential. Without ever asking what I did to call this situation upon me, my friend, I quote, said, "These kinds of problems are bound to happen to people who have solid morals. Don't think this will be the last one in your life. And don't pay too much heed to this noise, my friend. You are far more potent than this situation. Believe in your thoughts, don't be gaslit. We got your back. These are problems people face in foreign countries."

**Peace over Pay**

Finally, the company used this situation to get rid of me. They offered me two things: one was money—a lot of money—

to shut up, the other a more painstaking legal route to sue and be countersued. I chose the third: to ask for my arrears and salary for the notice period and leave. I didn't have an offer in hand. I had all the proofs of their wrongdoing, but I chose peace. They even said things to instigate a reaction from me, like that he had raped me or that I had seduced him for the money and visa sponsorship. Well, all of it stung, but their end game was to get rid of me. I posted my laptop and ID card, though I literally lived a stone's throw away from the office, and waited for my payout. At this point, a solicitor was appointed by them to mediate between us, again something new and intimidating, but I had to roll with it.

## Stepping Out of the Situation to Gain Perspective

I immediately left with a backpack to Scotland to clear my head, as it felt like the only pragmatic thing at that time. Though my relationship with my parents was sore, my sibling was dealing with her own problems. I didn't have issues like rent as I had utilised my father's guilt (for almost getting me married off to a psychopath) to get him to pay for a year's worth rent in Central London (bratty behaviour, I know). I met new people, lived a little.

During my backpacking expedition in Scotland, I met a New-York–based celebrity chef. She told me about how, many years ago when she was in her late 20s, she was approached by her then boss inappropriately and she jeopardised everything to be with him. Ultimately, he didn't leave his wife and children. In a way, she validated my judgement call, it felt just like the kind of story I wanted to hear. Especially since she came from a different cultural background and age demographic than mine, her acknowledgement carried significant weight. She mentioned that this was a common issue faced by women in the workforce, and given the age difference between us, her perspective felt especially validating. Hearing this from someone outside my own demographic made me realise that this problem is not new—it has likely persisted for decades, if not centuries.

Then why don't people find a solution to this? In hindsight, what my manager said made sense. He said that HR is literally in the back pockets of senior leadership. As threatening as it sounded at that point, the simple solution here could be to make HR departments a part of an autonomous nationalised body, including experts from the Labour Welfare Department, Women and Child Welfare and Corporate, a nationalised body that is not under the control of any private company. This should handle issues across industries, which will then ensure accountability regardless of the power and position of individuals in private sectors.

**Plight of the Whistle-Blower**

I realised this whole issue was about power dynamics. If you present anyone with the knife to jab you, there is a non-zero probability that they eventually will. Moral policing will only happen in the aftermath. So, when I was positioned as a single woman in a foreign country, in need of sponsorship, and without any family members around, even the most well-mannered of people were bound to show their dark side. That's how the world works. There are no Rams and Ravans today. It is just too much effort to find one's moral polarity and identify with it for life. One would rather function as per the situation or improvise. People have a spectrum of traits within themselves and they are well-aware of which traits get activated based on who, when, and where they are interacting with. So, the situation, the power dynamic, and the stakes were all that mattered. Eventually, after age, people are now talking about the atrocities they faced in this particular London-based telecom company, on Glassdoor and Reddit. The white CEO got publicly sacked for some legal suits against them in Europe.

It was then that I realised how powerful it really is sometimes to listen to your intuition. Calling out wrong for wrong may sound lonely and scary in the start, but it will inspire others to take action. Many people reached out to me saying what a brave thing I did and even tried to bait me into joining them to write a book to expose the company for their international wrongdoings. I simply refused everything, as I had realised you need to pick your friends carefully and your enemies even more carefully.

You often become the people you fight. My aspiration while relocating to London was to build my career. Never did it once interest me to take a short cut to pursue that. I eventually found a better designation with a Fortune 500 MNC, an amazing job profile, with a sensible manager (until he had to save his ass) and a much better pay. During that time, I felt lonely. I felt the judgement of so many people. I was hurt, depressed, and many things more. There were roommates and friends who were kind and did help me navigate the situation. So, life isn't all that unfair. If it gives you a problem, it will also offer you the necessary help to deal with it. Sometimes you need blind conviction in yourself and need to take the plunge.

## Life Lessons from the Other Side of Survival

Things I would have done differently now that I know better:

1. Research the company before accepting the offer.
2. Walk out at the first toxic encounter; don't ask advice from anyone.
3. Be clear, firm, and even a bit rude when you turn down unwanted sexual advances at workplace.
4. Don't consider your colleagues as friends, no room for emotions because people can weaponise everything

you say. Find neutral topics to be polite and banter, never show them the chink in your armour.

5. Build quality work relationships over quantity.
6. Keep a legal aid's number handy, take advice before reaching out to the HR. Because like we were informed, the HR (Grievance) truly is in the back pocket of the senior leadership.
7. Always trust your instinct and pen down unusual incidents in a journal or digitally, to ensure that when the shit hits the roof, you don't gaslight yourself or question your sanity.

So back to people handling, I don't think any one of them was evil in general. They were all just doing their job, even if morally it felt wrong. If the power dynamics weren't so skewed against me, then the company wouldn't be so audacious about their conduct with me. So, innately there are no good or bad people when it comes down to paying the bills, putting food on the table or saving for the kids' education. People will do the bloodiest things possible. If not this company, somewhere else, if not me, someone else, if not these bunch of idiots, another bunch. The bottom line is there are all sorts of problems one can face, some probably less severe than the one I just elaborated on, but if you don't go through it, you will never learn to handle people or situations. Even now I, like millions of women at work probably do, experience unwarranted attention at or outside of work, but I set **clear** and **firm** boundaries, because failing to do this will lead to unfortunate consequences. So yes, people are problematic but you have to know how much shit to take and when to stop. Each has their own threshold. It is when these are tested that you will need to take your own decisions based on your values and priorities at the time, long-term goals, short-term benefits, or even just basic instinct. No leader, book, friend, or therapist can really know what you are experiencing; you need to go deep and really know who you are to begin with. This takes a lot of solitude, time, and patience: to really know who you are and what your negotiables and non-negotiables are.

As a parting thought from this chapter: when you know your limitations, you become limitless!

# Chapter 3:
# Talent Plus Hard Work is Not Equal to Success

Your fancy Russell Group, Ivy League, IIT, or IIM degree can prepare you for frameworks, balance sheets, machine learning models, and case-study bullshit. What it **will never prepare you for** is the real battlefield: *people politics at work*. They don't teach you *Art of War* by Sun Tzu. They don't teach you emotional intelligence or Chanakyaniti. They don't teach survival in a jungle of fragile egos and hidden alliances. God forbid they train you in identifying a passive-aggressive narcissist pretending to be coworker.

**P for People Politics**

Let's break it down.

Talent is simply your ability to deliver what's written in your JD. Hard work is how you execute it—with integrity, initiative, and deadlines that keep you awake at night. Success? That's just the money and title they throw at you when you do the above *and* manage to not offend anyone with power.

So why is it never that simple?

Because we work with **people**, and human beings become the most unpredictable creatures when they're in survival mode, especially when shoved into artificially diverse teams where everyone brings their past trauma, ambition, insecurity, and entitlement into the same Zoom call. People don't respond to logic; they respond to their own wants and wounds. Even brilliant technical minds who've specialised for years in one vertical get blindsided because they don't understand the bigger political chessboard—reorgs (Organisational Restructuring), cancelled incentives, and shifting power dynamics. They internalise everything because no one gives them the context.

Senior executives don't bother explaining anything, and middle managers are too busy saving their own asses to enlighten the team. The ones suffering at the bottom are the most talented, ironically the best, but the least prepared.

**Colour, Colour, Which Colour Do You Choose?**

On top of this, let's address the **linguistic favouritism** that everyone pretends doesn't exist. Indian tech is a mini-subcontinent. People band together based on language and culture like mini clans. Hiring decisions often tilt toward the guy who speaks the same mother tongue as the interviewer/hiring manager. If two candidates are equal, the one who matches the cultural-linguistic bubble gets hired, unless the cheaper one is chosen to reduce the CTC burden. Meritocracy, my foot!

Then there's the **gendered division of labour**, still alive and thriving in November 2025. High-stakes, high-visibility roles magically get reserved for male counterparts because they're "more available" for odd time zones. Women? We get shunted into roles requiring emotional labour: listening to tantrums, arranging team outings, managing HR engagement, remembering birthdays, handling managers' frustrations. And this is **on top** of our actual jobs in product, data, coding, consulting, and analytics. Nobody says it directly but every woman knows she is expected to be the emotional sponge of the department.

Even in 2025, women are still hired for diversity stats but excluded from real decision-making: quarterly planning, budgeting, strategy, and stakeholder negotiations. The spirit of women in tech isn't just ignored; it's beaten into silence. Any woman who refuses this script, any feminist who holds boundaries, is labelled "difficult," "not a culture fit," or "too intense." The bar for being "likable" is basically "be agreeable or be gone."

### "Bro Code" Culture at Work

Meanwhile, the only universal bonding activity at work—the watercooler or smoke-break gossip—reveals everything about our so-called "evolved" white-collared professional ecosystem. Do highly educated engineers discuss the latest GPT model, Trump's foreign policy changes, or India's next unicorn? Hell no! Our evolutionary wiring hasn't changed: 90% of conversations are still about sex: lack of it, pursuit of it, or scandals involving it.

It's disappointing but true: male-dominated tech spaces are a circus of non-veg jokes, body-shaming, fantasising aloud about female colleagues, and mocking women's personal choices. Women are forced to either join in and tolerate this nonsense or isolate themselves until they find a safer tribe.

Office parties funded by venture capitalists or foreign stakeholders for better employee recreation and retreat purposes—worth lakhs of rupees—are often nothing but a setting with cheap liquor, dim lighting, and opportunities for people with power to approach people without power. Social pressure forces attendance, but moral boundaries crack under intoxication and hierarchy. This is why India ranks #2 in workplace romances [15], whether people are married or not. These relationships influence everything: visa sponsorships, layoffs, promotions, incentives. I'm not judging romance. I'm judging the system that forces people into dysfunctional power dynamics to survive office politics.

### Compulsive Over Conscious Relationships

Indian tech back offices, offshore centres, GCCs—all operate 12–18 hours per day on an average. Indian startups proudly stretch to 20+ hours. When you have no life outside work, you settle for convenient relationships, even unhealthy ones. Refuse them, and you're labelled anti-social or arrogant. Executive groups mirror this dynamic—golf buddies, tennis networking, Sunday brunch investor circles—interpersonal politics intertwined with professional power.

The middle-class, high-integrity, morally grounded folks? They suffer the most. They don't know how to navigate grey zones, don't play dirty, don't gossip strategically. They internalise, overthink, and burn out. The consequences sometimes explode as rage quitting, HR escalations, and lawsuits. But mostly these frustrations surface as anonymous Reddit rants, Glassdoor reviews, or impulsive job hops.

**Mental health support? A joke**

India lacks non-patriarchal, competent psychologists. Friends gossip, colleagues misinterpret, managers gaslight. So where does one get genuine emotional support to navigate workplace politics?

This is where mythology hits home.

*Shakuni won the war not with strength or skill, but with a rigged dice game because he knew the unbeatable Pandavas, with all their divine training and unmatched talent, lacked the cunning required to survive deception.*

Similarly, first-generation professionals—talented, hardworking, sincere—often lose not because they're incompetent, but because they're playing an honest game in a dishonest arena.

And no one trains us for that.

As much as we'd all love to believe that talent gets us through the right doors and hard work helps us stay there, that illusion needs to die a dignified death. It's neither. In the real world, for every one person who raises a moral concern at work, there are twenty others ready to do the heavy lifting, play work-dog, stay late, bend over backwards, and quietly absorb whatever nonsense comes their way.

So, when someone finally speaks up about unfairness—from overwork to bias to harassment—they're often dismissed as "too sensitive," "too dramatic," or "not a team player." The issue gets buried, the person gets labelled, and the world keeps spinning.

### What Can One Realistically Do?

If we insist on bringing more diversity into the workplace—more talent, more women, more thinkers and innovators—then we also need to make the workplace accommodating, not performative. You can't invite people to run a race that was designed by men, for men, timed around their bodies, expectations, availability, and social freedom... and then wonder why everyone else "isn't delivering."

**Talent doesn't fail.**

**The environment does.**

And unless companies redesign the game, not just the recruitment posters, they'll keep losing brilliant people, especially the ones who refuse to shrink themselves just to fit a mould they were never meant to fit.

# Chapter 4: Dealing with Conflict, Not Running from it

I have realised this: the people or situations that trigger you will haunt you until you turn around and face it. In different forms and shapes. For instance, you have an insecure, nagging, unhappy cat lady as your manager, whom you hate from the holiest part of your existence and think switching your job will help you find a better manager. Guess what, you will end up wasting time and energy in finding another job with an equally shoddy cat lady. Why? That's how energy works, whatever unfinished business you have, you will continue to vibrate in that frequency, because our minds can't deal with lack of closure. You will keep actively or passively seeking that situation again at a subconscious level. Allow me to walk you through.

### Let's Do a Quick Activity Together

Let's do the opposite of meditation; I call it self-torture or reliving trauma to ensure you force yourself to closure. Where ever you're reading this book—in a busy bus, while riding an uber to work, hiding it under your bench at a boring lecture (don't do that too many times, paid for it too), at the loo while doing your business or by the bedstand at the end of the day—imagine the most triggering, helpless feeling you have ever experienced, then think of the anticipation of that experience. For instance, you have been called to the principal's office in the middle of a school day, and you see your father's car pulled up in the school parking lot. As a South Asian kid, my body can already feel the aftermath of that meeting. Or think of a weekly one-on-one so toxic that your manager is **gaslighting** you every week into believing you are one of the most worthless fuckers on earth. Or the moment you hear the notification on your mobile from your partner who has been a bit aloof of late, that reads, "We need to talk." Now think of the moments/ hours/days between knowing shit is about to go down and the actual onset of the event. That 2-minute walk with the school peon from the classroom to the principal's office, the weekend before another of those toxic one-on-ones with your pain-in-the-ass manager. Those fleeting moments between knowing your partner needs to "talk to you" and actually talking. Those are the worst, most hellish moments of one's life. Not only that, when you go through with it nobody rewards you for this Everest climbing, freaky, near-death experience. The world just goes on. The body chemicals go through a whole roller coaster: fear, anxiety, guilt, shame, sadness. You end up praying to everything you consider holy, even the most atheistic person can agree we end up experiencing the divine at this point. Now picture this: in a few year, this situation might or might not impact you. For instance, if you don't control your emotions with your manager, you might end up losing a job which might plunge you deeper into debt, it might have a domino effect in your personal life, lose your visa and end up jobless in your parent's home for a good year (based on true incidents). So no, don't let the internet and western psychologists **trivialise your struggle**. Yeah, it's not a 9/11 terrorist attack, you're not George Bush giving a speech at an elementary school who just heard about the news in front of a class full of cute, innocent American kids, but your problems matter too. To whom? To you! Why are everyday problems brushed under the carpet as "chill, it will be alright"? No, buddy, you fucking don't know if it will. If this person had staked everything in life and lost it all with control in their very own hands, they would not dare give this nonchalant advice. You don't know squat, so don't walk into Chapter 24 and judge me!

## Your Problems are a Big Deal!

So, give a shit about your problems, not in a way that will spiral into a negative hell hole, but in a pragmatic problem-solving method. Take it as seriously as you took the damn school board exams or some random India versus Pakistan last over, last ball situation. Yes, it matters. One wrong word, one wrong move will affect you, sabotage your progress, and confidence. Nobody gives a shit, but you do and you should. It is your life. Your micro success, micro failure though unnoticed, matter in shaping every cell in your body, eventually your future generations. So, whatever the situation be, I won't preach, but I can tell you what I have always done, even from the tender ages of 6 or 7 when I was strategically and systematically targeted by my private secondary education board school for being the only dark skinned, black sheep girl student from a non-affluent family. All the mischief ever was pinned on me, because the other parents donated 200% more than my parents could afford, so their kids could never be schooled or blamed for their wrongdoing. Although I would ask for help, my parents would turn a blind eye because they couldn't afford another school change; after all, money matters. I would turn to the highest power possible, something supreme, something beyond the understanding of normal mortal brains, walk in to defend myself, brave the wooden scale whacking or blatant slaps on my tender face or worse, the tag of being called a thief, liar, or what not. At that moment, the self-centred mind would tell me, "This is all happening to you because people hate you." Well, in reality, none of those people give two shits about what they did to you.

It was mostly, the principal sucking up to whoever could afford higher donations, even if that meant scarring an innocent child for life. I would tap into that divine frequency and walk through whatever it was in full awareness. Yet a higher autopilot where words of defense, counter arguments, and truth would sometimes escalate matters, sometimes resolve issues, but would either way liberate me, because I would stand by the truth. And whatever has to unfold will unfold eventually; it's the fear of anticipation that kills our self-confidence amputating us before we face the real battle. It's like walking out of a battle field with a severed shoulder, that happened because your arrow back fired. All it takes is courage and a little bit of impatience. Don't listen to bullshit 19th century advice on patience, the people who wrote those lines are all turning in their graves knowing they are outdated. This is a capitalist world driven only by motives that can make people rich, keep them rich, in power or relevant; every other feeling of injustice, or moralistic bullshit that the helpless and poor speak about is just a loser's whine.

**Identify Gaslighting at Work**

For instance, while I was working for this MNC, I had the most humble, emotionally stable, millennial manager whom I was thankful to have. Until his own job and his unborn child's future was at stake. He then turned into a mind-fucking cruel nasty manager who put me under systematic stress so that I ended up succumbing to fatty liver and hypothyroidism. Which again proves my point: if someone or something has a tendency towards something, external factors like stress would accelerate that tendency further. This experience was right after my horrible experience at the telecom company with that misogynistic dimwit. I had almost lost hope that there were decent coworkers around. That's when, after six months of relentless job hunting and soul searching, I found this MNC. I didn't realise I was going through such a bad time until I wasn't. This company celebrated me for my talent, my cerebral abilities, and here, my manager was just about my age and one of kindest, most humble guys I have met. No, this was not a relatively better experience; it was indeed an honest better work environment and working relationship with my higher-up.

I was able to fully utilise my knowledge as a newly post graduated Data Scientist, combine it with my entrepreneurial creative streak, and bring structure with my management experience from my past. This role was every reason I had picked Data Product Management. They even went an extra mile and wrote an entire LinkedIn post with my headshot and introduction as if I was some kind of an important resource. I was handed over the most crucial database in the organisation with sensitive health data of celebrity fighters. I could strategise the governance, develop dashboards, create new views of the data. I was in charge and I was loving the autonomy.

My manager was such a chill guy that he didn't care unless I had an escalation. He was the opposite of misogynist, happily married and had the kindest approach to dealing with problems. Until there came a point when the organisation was getting restructured, and they had to strategically let go of people without making us feel it was an ethnic filtration. Up until then, I didn't even realise the team comprised of different skin types, different linguistic abilities, and different genders. It was when the shit got real for them, which was much earlier than shit hitting us. We, when I say we, I really mean the non-white immigrant team members who needed visa sponsorship, who were being targeted not in the direct "you're brown so leave" sort of way, but in the most subtle British way as one could.

My then manager was accusing me of bringing my fully Indian accent onto work calls, which confused and disturbed the American clients on call (who had written page long appreciation emails about how wonderful my contribution had been to their organisation). I was also told my approach (which until then was structured, professional, and get-it-done) was too loud, blatant, and lacked basic etiquette. I was asked if in India they failed to teach us how to knock on meeting doors before entering. I was even asked why I didn't mingle outside of work with our freshly divorced senior manager. I know all this sounds like another story of office sexual harassment of sorts, but trust me, this was all staged. They were trying to get us to rage quit.

Why?

Because the organisation was going through a major organisational restructure where the client had proposed to retain only the necessary staff. And naturally, the coloured immigrant population, as in most foreign countries, was handling the important, buck-getting, buck-saving, buck-retaining jobs at the price of peanuts. So, when the initial list of go/no-go list of redundancy was announced, the majority of them were white, including the freshly divorced maniac, the kind manager and others, because they all drew salaries that afforded them at least a Tesla and a Merc, while owning homes in London, whereas we scraped the bottom trying to make rent, cover the cost of living, and student loans.

**Connecting the Dots in a Blind Spot**

Slowly, the Jira board started looking different. All the Jira tasks, stories and epics (refer to Glossary) owned by the brown folks started being bulk edited into our white managers' names. All the product insights and domain knowledge we had gathered during our course was being documented in the name of being well-accounted for. More and more meetings were being held, where we were slowly gaslit into believing we were doing a bad job or we didn't deserve the role, so that we either rage quit or accepted to go into performance review, suffer some more, and then quit. When some of us started documenting the feedback from one session to another, started maintaining email proof of our work, and started gathering evidence of our efficiency, we were put on gardening leave. It was one of the craziest mind-bending shit I have experienced.

I should truly give it to the British, they really know how to terrorise people in the most subtle manner. No wonder half the world was colonised by them for so many fucking centuries. People don't realise their brutality until it's too late, haha! No wonder their military is undefeated; they really decapacitate their enemies mentally and psychologically, even before the physical war begins.

Man, in those 6 months, during the first 3 months I really ended up succumbing to their rubbish. It was when I had a work trip to the USA, that I took some time off.. I backpacked through the Rocky Mountains with a bunch of elderly Americans; I discussed this and everything else with them. I had like a slice of life experience with them and a break from everything. That's when I realised there was nothing wrong with me. Also, during my client visit to the company's headquarters, I had the chance to meet the decision-makers, who really had a problem with my managers back in UK. The sly, subtle brutality of the British couldn't beat the directness of the Americans. They just refused lunch invitations, renewal meeting invites, future contracts, and simply warned them of a massive lay-off. It was then that I gained my power back. Post this work charade, I whisked off to my backpacking trek adventure, which helped me connect the dots. This gave me time to digest what was what. It left me baffled and with a firsthand understanding of the plight of the colonised countries. The British are excellent at playing and winning mind games. I didn't hate anyone at this point, not the manager, not his senior, not the client. This time, I knew what I was up against: people's livelihood. I didn't want to rage quit, so I decided to immunise myself to these tricks, and at the same time, apply for jobs outside this organisation.

## Crisis Management and Quick Decision-Making

By the time I returned, I had this newfound confidence that I can handle shit. I went back to work only to realise they started a new angle of wanting me to go into "Performance Improvement Plan", without any acknowledgement to the amount of mental torture and unfairness they had subjected us to so far. My ask was if this would ensure job security or at least a visa sponsorship, as at this point, I was on Post-Study Work visa and needed to convert it into a work visa in another 12 months. I took an intelligent guess that if they do put me on a Performance Improvement Plan (PIP) and I do pass, what was the guarantee they would not fuck me over at the time of visa sponsorship? They sure seemed to have a pattern. I made these decisions subconsciously, but when the meeting was going on (one of those stressful one-to-one sessions with the subtly evil manager, who was previously my benchmark for kindness), I made a decision on the fly. The factors influencing my well-being were:

**My well-being = Job Security + Visa Sponsorship + Decent working relationships.**

Based on their pattern, none of these seemed solid, so I took the call that if I quit immediately, I would have the next 12 months to find a new job and pass probation (which is usually around 6 months). Given I was a product manager at this point, more so I could build a strong rapport at work which would eventually get work done without too many roadblocks. With this conviction, some savings, the remaining arrears and garden leave payout I decided to start making applications again for new jobs.

## Impact of Strategic Corporate Bullying

I was still hurting from the mental torture and torment, which lead to overeating and eventually lead to health issues like thyroid and fatty liver. The hurt these corporate cogs do to normal people is personal and brutal. There are of course labour laws to fight against them but how many times? What really remains at the end of the fight? This is why there should be centralisation of Human Resource (Grievance) and have regulations internationally, so employees are not exploited. Most of the immigrant population is so engrossed in survival that they don't get the time or chance to voice these concerns. Even if they do ask the simple, "Who asked you to come here and work? Go back to your home country," is a very paralysing response one isn't ready to receive.

**At the end of all this I realised:**

1. Feedback is not always to be internalised; assess who is providing it and if they are they qualified? Do they have the best of intentions? Are they in position of desperation? Do they have ulterior motives?

2. The post-colonial hangover has led us to believe we are lacking, that we are somehow at fault because that was how the colonisers got away with everything. This is so deeply rooted in our minds that it takes a lot of "un-conditioning" to understand that the world is still being colonised by the capitalists.

3. Building business acumen about the kind of acquisitions, restructures, domain, industry, work culture will be so much more important to ride the tough waves than just core skills. Because core skills make you think of staying till they ask you to leave; soft skills, domain expertise, and acumen for business train you to know when to leave at your own discretion.

4. Work on your skills, keep track of your progress at work and outside, always stay on the market. This helps you build innate confidence not only on your skills

but also on the market conditions in your industry. Talking to people about your problems in a problem-solving tone builds credibility. Find mentors and build networks. Networking is not knowing people, it's about people knowing you. Talk to people outside your organisation, have industry allies, during good and bad times, so that you not only have perspective, you also have a safe space to rant without jeopardising your existing work relationships.

All in all, conflict is inevitable—especially when the stakes are high and there is power or/and money on the table. *Lord Krishna literally took the pain of narrating an entire 18-chapter long tutorial on conflict resolution in the Bhagwad Gita.* If that doesn't prove the need and normalcy of this skill, then I doubt anything else could. The rule of thumb is to expect problems, prepare for them, navigate with grace, and resist the temptation to see yourself as a victim. Playing the victim may help you survive a moment, but it rarely helps you scale to the next level of achievement.

The wiser approach is to meet conflict with a calm yet fierce, stoic yet nuanced mindset—something that takes time and deliberate practice. Not every situation deserves an emotional response or a direct fight. Sometimes, the real strength lies in having enough awareness to exit gracefully, carry the lesson forward, and move on stronger than before.

Quoting the *Bhagavad Gita*, "The path to peace does not bypass struggle; it moves through it. **Conflict cannot be eliminated, only understood and navigated—with tact, discernment, and wisdom rather than brute force or ego.**"

# Chapter 5:
# CTC - Taxes - PF - Cost of Living = Peanuts

Let's be honest: the **primary reason** most of us cling to the tech industry is the pay check. Not passion. Not curiosity. Not some romantic dream of building the next big platform. It's simple math. **Five to six out of the ten highest-paying jobs in India** sit inside AI/Data, Software Engineering, Cybersecurity, Consulting, or Product [7]. The numbers alone are enough to funnel millions of young people into tech—even when half of them don't care about tech in the first place.

India is a middle-class country, and middle class in real income terms means **₹500,000 – ₹3 million per annum [8].** That's the sweet spot every multinational loves to exploit. These are the people who show loyalty, stay longer, tolerate the bullshit, defend the company on Glassdoor—because their lifestyle, home loans, EMIs, weddings and aging parents depend on that salary crediting on the last working day of every month.

But this equation is changing.

Gen Z isn't built like the millennials or Gen X. They're choosing independence over stability. **Only 16% of Indian Gen Z prefer a traditional, single full-time job; many combine work with side hustles [9].**They don't aspire to be corporate loyalists; they aspire to be *free*. They'll tolerate the traditional tech company for maybe **five years**—just long enough to observe the industry, build networks, study the psychology of managers, learn the loopholes, save some money, and then venture out.

And the stats confirm it:

While precise five-year company-retention figures are scarce, multiple Indian workforce surveys indicate **high early-career turnover among Gen Z**, with many planning to leave roles within the first few years in search of flexibility, better pay, or diversified career paths [9].

This massive dip shows two things:

1. Compensation and benefits are no longer enough.
2. Today's mid-senior professionals have higher appetite for risk, opportunity, and leadership outside corporate hierarchies.

Which means the traditional tech giants need to wake the fuck up. You cannot expect young people to come, absorb toxicity, follow broken processes, and then magically evolve into the ethical, empathetic founders of tomorrow. Any scarring experience they face as freshers—humiliation, gaslighting, bully managers—will either:

**a)** turn them into the same monsters later, or

**b)** give them such aversion that they'll build companies deliberately rejecting anything that resembles corporate cruelty.

Either way, it impacts the industry's future.

Companies need to move toward **process-oriented, ego-free operations**, not personality-driven fiefdoms. Reduce dependency on individuals and their tantrums, and you automatically improve collaboration, stability, and innovation. Humility at work is not a luxury; it's the foundation of sustainable talent retention.

Now let's address the salary myth.

There is a **massive** variance even within tech. The core difference?

## Product Companies vs. Service Companies

Product companies make money from selling their product—SKUs, subscriptions, features, licenses. The profit per employee is high. They hire fewer people but higher-quality talent. Innovation is the goal. Expertise is valued.

**Examples: Meta, Salesforce, Google**

Their Achilles heel? Market monopoly. OS is dominated by Microsoft, Apple, and Linux. Breaking into that space requires an insane price or performance disruption. China could launch Kylin. India could launch Bharat OS. But for most, this is an impenetrable fortress.

On the other hand, **Service companies** make money from hours. Billable hours. Project hours. Human hours.

**Accenture, TCS, Wipro, Infosys, Cognizant, HCL**—basically every name plastered from Bellandur flyover to ITPL.

90% of the Indian tech industry is service-based. So, their profit increases only when two things increase:

**Number of employees × hours squeezed out of them.**

This is why they mass hire like there's no tomorrow. Time is money. People are cost centres. Attrition is expected. Promotions are slow. Salaries stagnate.

This is the brutal structure of Indian tech.

Not good or bad—**just the truth we operate in.**

The IT billing models used across India's service industry don't just decide revenue for companies: they silently dictate the **quality of life, salaries, and sanity** of every employee trapped inside the system. These models are the invisible puppeteers controlling workload, deadlines, hiring strategies, and profit margins. And like every puppet show, the audience rarely sees the strings.

Here are the billing models that rule Indian IT [6]:

**1. Time & Material (T&M)**

Clients are billed for every hour an employee breathes in the direction of work. Add to that the "operational costs"—workspace, software licenses, laptops, training programmes, "employee well-being" initiatives, the entire melodrama.

This model thrives in projects where requirements mutate every week. It's flexible, scalable, and the most profitable when the project has no end in sight. Chaos = Cash.

**2. Fixed Price Model**

Here, the client pays for a predetermined scope. The company estimates the humans, machines, hours, and effort needed and slaps a price on it.

Clients love the predictability; companies hate the rigidity.

Any change becomes a **Change Request (CR),** which is basically corporate daylight robbery, politely invoiced.

**3. Fixed Deliverable/Fixed Time Model**

This one bills clients by milestones: "Deliver feature X by date Y."

It's slightly more flexible than Fixed Price but still conservative.

Risk is balanced:

- If the client delays inputs, the company suffers.
- If the company screws up timelines, the client bleeds patience.
- Scope changes are tolerated only if they fit inside the holy timeline.

### 4. Hybrid Models

A mix of T&M and Fixed Price, or T&M and Milestone-based billing.

A patchwork quilt of everything.

The Frankenstein model of IT billing.

But the real scam—the core outrage—lies in what companies charge **versus** what employees earn.

Regardless of the billing model, clients are charged an amount that is often **100× the actual employee cost**.

Employees are priced like exotic commodities:

- Degree
- Pedigree
- Skillset
- Years of experience
- Role

Each becomes a multiplier on an already inflated rate card.

These rate cards are guarded like family jewels by sales and pre-sales teams, because that's where the **real money** is made.

### Let's Talk About Freshers/Junior Resources

Fresh graduates from Tier 1 cities—non-IIT—join at **₹300,000 –₹800,000 per year, as of 2025 [10].**

Except, to foreign clients, they're presented as "mid-level consultants" and billed at **₹3 million – ₹7 million per year [10].**

That's a profit margin of almost **99%**.

**Now the mid-senior hires.**

Employees earning **₹2 million – ₹5 million per year [10]** are made to shoulder the workload of two people because AI has automated the grunt work, so they're now expected to "move up the value chain."

Clients are billed **₹10 million – ₹20 million per year** for these same employees.

A neat 80% margin.

This is how Indian IT giants show "record profits" every year, squeezing more out of the same human.

**And here's the lesser-known scandal:**

Most foreign clients allocate additional budgets specifically for:

- team outings
- wellness programmes
- mental health support
- fitness memberships
- engagement activities
- training and upskilling

These funds never reach employees.

Middle managers quietly swallow them.

Fake bills, bloated invoices, creative accounting: you name it.

Employees get a stale Domino's pizza party once a year and are expected to clap like seals.

Mid-sized companies, especially, love this trick—pocketing wellness funds to artificially plump up their balance sheets and appear "high-growth" to investors and auditors, while their actual core business performance is mediocre at best.

The irony?

Most employees don't even know these budgets exist.

They're scammed without ever realising they were supposed to receive something in the first place.

Over the last 20 years, the entire billing landscape has started shifting. The once-worshipped **T&M** model—which used to dominate at **68.2%** among Indian IT service providers—has crashed down to around **35%** today [11].

**But why?**

Because clients have woken the hell up. They want **accountability**, not inflated hourly billing. They want **transparency**, not a never-ending tap running into the pockets of service giants.

This demand for clearer, fairer pricing has forced service providers to Frankenstein their models. Most large-scale projects today run on **Hybrid Billing**—a fixed price model for predictable, asset-heavy parts of the project, and a T&M model for the volatile or exploratory components. It's no longer a clean cut; it's a stitched-together survival tactic.

But the real earthquake in this ecosystem has been the arrival of **generative AI**.

In the last three years alone, GenAI has detonated every traditional assumption. Clients now prefer hiring **one strong senior resource** who is able to leverage AI tools to expedite their work and efficiency of delivering than working in silos.

These tools allow a single experienced engineer to deliver the work of **two or three juniors** with better quality, faster turnaround, and deeper domain intuition. Suddenly, domain expertise plus AI augmentation is more valuable than throwing a room full of juniors at the problem.

This completely breaks the traditional Indian service provider model, which has historically depended on **cheap junior labour** to maximise profit margins. That era is dying. Slowly, but very clearly.

On top of that, AI-driven solution accelerators like reusable frameworks, platform templates, and workflow automations are offering clients **fixed price** or **milestone-based** proposals that are far more attractive than T&M. When a system can auto-generate documentation, code skeletons, test cases, migrations, or architecture drafts, why pay for a human's hour-by-hour presence?

Clients don't want to pay for warm bodies anymore; they want results.

And AI gives them exactly that—with no HR overhead, no payroll, no sick leave, no training, no attrition.

So, what will really be Indian Tech's leverage if their cost-effective delivery centres, unchartered working hours, and unlimited access to fresh talent can be replaced by an existing worker who integrates their experience and domain knowledge with the power of AI? Fodder for thought!

# Chapter 6: Bitter or Better

By now, we've peeled back enough layers to see the rotting machinery underneath the shiny, global tech façade. We've seen how volatile the industry is—from Silicon Valley to Bengaluru, from London to Hyderabad. We've seen how India and the West share an uncomfortable similarity: a deep, systemic toxicity that thrives on insecurity, ego-driven leadership, and an industrialised hire-and-fire culture where employees are little more than headcounts on a spreadsheet. We've exposed how talent alone won't save you. We've mapped how culture, regional favouritism, cliques, and corporate caste systems play a far bigger role in shaping careers than any résumé bullet point.

**So, what does all this actually lead to?**

It leads to the quietest and most widespread epidemic of modern India—**internalised mental illness.**

The kind that doesn't announce itself through public breakdowns or dramatic scenes. Instead, it nestles deep in the body, showing up as fatty liver in a 28-year-old, hypertension in a 31-year-old, unexplained heart palpitations in a 35-year-old, insomnia in someone who doesn't drink, migraines in someone who barely leaves their desk, and elevated anxiety in someone who "has nothing to be anxious about."

These illnesses don't remain contained. They leak. They seep into homes. They distort marriages. They widen emotional gaps between partners. They silently shape children who grow up either watching parents scream at each other or watching parents who barely speak at all.

**This is the real cost of the modern workplace.**

Most people today, especially in tech, are lonely in crowds. They walk into office buildings filled with hundreds of people, yet feel completely unseen. They spend their days toggling between Jira boards, Slack messages, Zoom calls, and tight deadlines. They eat standing up, gym mechanically, drink on weekends, scroll away their nights, travel occasionally, and maintain relationships that are more "functional" than fulfilling.

Beneath the curated lives on Instagram lies a heavy, constant pressure, the kind that comes from internalising office politics, absorbing passive-aggressive comments, and convincing yourself that every criticism is a personal failure. The worst part? Most of this "feedback" is not constructive; it's often disguised insecurity, weaponised by managers who were never trained to lead and colleagues who fear competition.

When the pressure becomes unbearable, people resort to short-term coping: rage posts on Reddit and X, anonymous confessions on Blind, frantic job switching, and spontaneous resignations. It feels good for a few hours. Then the cycle starts again. The wound doesn't heal; the wallpaper simply changes.

**Never Ending Loop of Misery**

Like I said in the prologue:

**If you prematurely exit one reality without learning your lesson, you simply re-enter another version of the same karmic classroom. Different people, same pattern. Different company, same idiot in a different shirt. Different city, same lesson with a new accent.**

The universe is funny that way.

It doesn't promote you because you ran.

It promotes you because you evolved.

Only when you truly integrate the lesson—when your self-worth is no longer held hostage by your job, when you stop outsourcing validation to managers, when you see through the masks—does your reality shift.

Otherwise, the cycle repeats endlessly:

In every job.

In every relationship.

In every version of your life.

Across timelines, across metaverses.

But let's be brutally honest. The people who suffer the most are the ones with responsibilities. The ones with aging parents, EMIs, school fees, marriages in negotiation phases, extended family expectations, and a deep terror of financial instability. These are the employees who cannot walk away. And corporate machinery knows that.

Those so-called "caring" one-on-one meetings?

Often they're not for concern—they're reconnaissance missions.

Managers ask about your personal life not to support you but to map your vulnerabilities.

Are you the sole earner?

Are you taking care of loved ones?

Do you have medical bills?

Are you desperate to keep your visa?

Are you terrified of losing the job?

In the wrong hands, this information becomes ammunition.

Let's stop sugar-coating this:

**Corporate is not family. Corporate is Kurukshetra, a battlefield.**

Every meeting is a war council.

Every appraisal cycle is a test of survival.

Every project is a siege with unrealistic deadlines disguised as "aggressive targets."

And in war, empathy is often a tactic—not a principle.

People show kindness when it helps them maintain power.

Over time, when there's no escape route and your back is against the wall, your body begins to revolt. It starts sending alarms: palpitations, digestive issues, panic attacks, numbness, brain fog, sudden tears during lunch breaks, disproportionate rage, inability to concentrate. These aren't "mood swings." These are distress signals from a system pushed beyond its limit.

This collapse is not limited to "weak people"—it's happening across genders, across income brackets, across age groups. The most common victims are between 22 and 45—the prime working years.

And the fallout doesn't stop there. When one person breaks down, their entire household feels the ripple. If both partners are suffering under toxic workplaces, their relationship turns into an emotional war zone. Children raised in this atmosphere grow up either hyper-independent or emotionally fragile. Trauma trickles down, quietly, generationally.

But there's another side too—the exception, the anomaly, the rebel narrative.

People who aren't bound by responsibilities, no kids, no spouse, no dependent parents, sometimes use toxic workplaces as *fuel.* They convert frustration into fire. They quit without fear. They switch fields. They build businesses. They freelance. They experiment. They fail forward. They take the path of risk, not because it is romantic, but because they have nothing to lose.

For them, toxic workplaces become catalysts.

For others, curses.

The outcome depends entirely on age, support systems, emotional resilience, and risk appetite.

But here's the absolute truth:

**Toxic environments don't leave anyone unchanged.**

Everyone is sculpted by the battles they fight at work.

Some emerge sharper, wiser.

Some emerge bitter, bruised.

Some emerge broken.

Some emerge reborn.

Work either breaks you or remakes you.

And how you respond becomes the turning point of your life.

Which is why, in this chapter, I want to give you the three core strategies that saved me—strategies forged through my own battles across India, the UK, service companies, startups, global clients, narcissistic leadership, bias, and betrayal.

I call them the **SSS Strategies**:

**Speak. Switch. Startup.**

Nothing revolutionary.

Nothing poetic.

Just brutally practical.

Now, let's break each one down, with the tools, risks, techniques, and mindset you need to execute them.

**Strategy 1: SPEAK**

Before we even enter the arena of "Switch" or "Startup," we begin with the most difficult, uncomfortable, deeply human strategy: **Speak**.

Contrary to popular belief, speaking up is not the last resort, it is the first purification ritual. Negotiation is first diplomatic move of any conflict, even wars. *Remember how India's great diplomats like Hanuman were first sent to Ravana's court to negotiate terms of peace with dialogue.*

Conflict isn't the problem; silence is. Silence is where resentment grows mould, where misunderstanding multiplies, where bullies thrive.

Speaking is not shouting.

Speaking is not gossip.

Speaking is not venting to the wrong people.

Speaking is **clarity**.

**Step 1: Speak to the person causing the issue—directly, cleanly, and factually.**

Most people, when someone annoys or disrespects them, run to colleagues and start whispering. Gossiping feels cathartic, but it's the fastest way to ruin your reputation *and* worsen the other person's behaviour. Once the Chinese whispers reach them, usually distorted, they double down, even if they weren't originally malicious.

So instead, you start simple:

1. **Draft an unsent email or Slack message.**
2. Describe the incident(s): when, what, how—with zero emotional adjectives.
3. Facts only.
4. **Explain how it affected your work.**

   Not your ego, not your mood—your *work*.

   Because work is the only language corporations understand.
5. **State your expectation of correction.**

   Calm. Crisp. Boundary-setting.

Something like:

"Hey, during X meeting on Y date, the comment about Z affected ABC part of the project. I'd like us to realign so this doesn't repeat. Can we discuss?"

Friendly tone, steel spine.

This does three powerful things:

- It signals: **I'm not your doormat.**
- It forces accountability: **You will be held responsible for your actions.**
- It sets clarity: **These are my boundaries. Respect them.**

And you do this privately. Not in a group call, not as public humiliation, unless someone is chronically abusive, in which case public assertiveness becomes necessary.

Give them a chance to correct themselves. Many people genuinely don't realise when they've crossed a line. Others do, but a direct, documented note forces them to behave.

Offering a follow-up call—a coffee chat or a quick Zoom—allows them space to clarify or apologise. If they take that chance, great. You've both grown.

If not?

Now you escalate—strategically.

**Step 2: If speaking doesn't work, involve the People Manager, not HR.**

Let's be brutally honest here.

**HR is not your friend. HR is a shield for senior leadership.**

HR exists to protect the company, not you.

They are a cost centre, not a power centre.

Going to HR without ironclad evidence is like walking into a lion's den wearing deodorant made of chicken broth.

Most HR departments will gaslight you with "have you tried communicating?" or "we'll mediate" and then conveniently bury the issue. Meanwhile, your manager—the one causing the problem—is already sipping chai with the HR Business Partner, discussing how you are "too emotional," "too sensitive," or "not a culture fit."

One of previous employers literally told me to my face (after making an unwarranted sexual advance which I refuted):

**"Escalate to HR department if you want to. They're in the pockets of the company's senior leadership. *I am senior leadership.*"**

With chills running down my spine, that was the day I realised: corporate justice is not justice—it's politics.

So instead of running to HR unarmed, you:

**Step 3: DOCUMENT EVERYTHING.**

Not in a notebook. Not on your office desktop.

In a **cloud-based, personal, private digital journal**.

Record:

- Incidents
- Dates and timestamps
- Screenshots (with metadata)
- Voice memos
- Photos
- Witness presence
- Mails

Keep everything meticulously organised.

This is not paranoia. This is insurance.

*Like the Pandavas collecting allies, weapons, and strategies before confronting the Kauravas, you are preparing your armour for the eventual confrontation.*

**Step 4: If the issue is harassment or severe toxicity, get external legal advice.**

Not from your friend who once read a PDF on labour laws.

Not from your boss's boss who "will look into it."

A real lawyer.

A one-hour consultation with a labour-law professional can save your entire career. They will tell you:

- What rights you actually have
- Whether you have a fighting case

- What documentation is required
- How to phrase your escalation
- What to avoid
- How to protect yourself

Sometimes, even knowing your rights gives you the confidence to respond differently.

**Step 5: If you are mentally collapsing, seek paid mental health support.**

Not your co-worker.

Not your cousin.

Not your friend at 2 a.m.

Not ChatGPT.

Not Google.

**A real therapist.**

And please—for your own safety—don't use AI tools to dump your trauma. You're creating a digital persona of your deepest vulnerabilities. There are no guardrails protecting you from a future data breach.

Platforms like **Practo** in India offer 100% confidential therapy sessions for approx. ₹1100/hour. Many therapists offer free follow-up calls. Consider this an investment, not an expense.

Your mind is your battlefield.

You cannot fight if you are bleeding internally.

**The real point of SPEAK:**

You're not trying to win arguments.

You're trying to reclaim power.

Speaking:

- Breaks fear
- Breaks patterns
- Breaks illusions
- Breaks manipulation

And restores your spine.

If done correctly, it can transform your entire workplace dynamic.

If done unsuccessfully, it becomes the foundation for the next strategy–**Switch**.

**Strategy 2: SWITCH**

If speaking didn't work or worked only partially, you enter the second strategy: **Switch**.

Switching is not escapism. It is strategic migration–*like the Pandavas leaving Hastinapura not out of weakness but to build their strength in the forests, to find new allies, to sharpen their weapons, and to eventually return with clarity, to annex their rightful place on the throne.*

Switching is a dignified exit.

A conscious realignment.

A reclamation of your destiny.

And you don't wait until you're completely broken.

You switch **while you still have strength**.

**Step 1: Keep therapy going.**

If you started mental health support in the Speak phase–continue.

Switching requires clarity, not desperation.

If you haven't started: do it now.

A therapist becomes your sounding board, your mirror, your grounding force.

They help you process:

- The trauma of the old job
- Your patterns
- Your blind spots
- Your coping style
- Your triggers
- Your real desires
- The type of team you thrive in
- The type of work that drains you

You don't want to repeat the same karmic loop in a new office with a different logo.

**Step 2: Go outside your corporate bubble.**

Now you begin something that most Indian employees (especially the introverted tech crowd) avoid—**real-world community.**

You step outside office walls.

Into spaces where your identity is not defined by your designation.

Join places where you can learn complementary skills:

- Toastmasters International
- Bengaluru tech meetups (Meetup app, Luma, Airtribe, Foyer, TPF events)

- Product communities
- AI communities
- Design meetups
- Hackathons
- Public speaking clubs
- Founder circles
- Women-in-tech circles

Why?

Because networking done correctly is not about begging for referrals.

It is about building a **tribe of thinkers** who uplift each other.

When you enter these rooms not as "X from Y company" but as *yourself*, you expand your sense of possibility. You hear stories, find mentors, discover parallel paths, and realise that your workplace was not "the world", it was just a badly designed simulation you were trapped in.

**Step 3: Upgrade your skill stack—strategically, not desperately.**

Every toxic workplace convinces you that you are incompetent.

Every good workplace convinces you that you are unstoppable.

So, you need to know who you TRULY are.

And the only way to know that is through exploration.

Use your evenings or weekends (instead of doom-scrolling) to:

- Take micro-courses

- Experiment with new tools
- Learn generative AI workflows
- Explore one speciality deeply
- Learn complementary soft skills
- Read industry whitepapers
- Write small LinkedIn posts about your insights

Your goal is not to become a "jack of all trades."

Your goal is to become **multidimensional,** not multi-confused.

Pick **one area you could work in even if nobody paid you.**

That's your creative baseline.

Then pick **one area the industry values**, even if it's not romantic.

That's your income engine.

Where these two intersect: that's your sweet spot.

**Step 4: Keep a running record of your ideas.**

LinkedIn is your friend if you use it correctly:

- Write insights
- Summarise your learnings
- Talk about your industry
- Share your opinions
- Post your research
- Collaborate with thinkers
- Amplify your voice

You are not showing off.

You are documenting your evolution.

You are training the algorithm to bring opportunities to you.

Platforms like Medium, Reddit (professionally), and GitHub are tools of visibility.

**Step 5: Apply with intention, not desperation.**

Switching is not:

"Let me apply to 100 jobs a day and pray."

Switching is:

"I know exactly what I want next, **and** what I will NEVER tolerate again."

When switching, your goal is not only to find a role.

It is to find a **new karmic timeline**.

A new environment where your nervous system can breathe.

A place where you don't walk into the office already half-dead.

Switching is your rebirth.

Don't rush your reincarnation.

**Strategy 3: STARTUP**

Let's be honest, most people romanticise entrepreneurship without understanding its brutality.

But if you have:

- No big financial responsibilities
- No dependents

- A reasonable savings runway
- A burning idea
- The inability to tolerate toxicity anymore
- The urge to build
- The instinct to create

Then entrepreneurship becomes a viable, even powerful exit path.

This is not the path of comfort.

This is the path of *Dharma.*

*Like Rama walking into exile–he didn't choose comfort, he chose alignment.*

**Step 1: Prepare your psychological safety net.**

Before you resign in a fit of rage or triumph:

- Build at least **8–12 months** of savings
- Clear urgent debts
- Calculate your burn rate
- Know your bare minimum survival expenses
- Inform no one except 1–2 trusted advisors
- Build in silence

This safety net stops you from making desperate, stupid decisions.

**Step 2: DO NOT start building the product first.**

Every techie's first mistake:

"I'll build an app. Then customers will come."

No.

Stop.

Take a deep breath.

Building first is like running into war without armour.

Start with a **Lean Canvas**.

A one-page business plan that forces you to answer:

- What problem am I solving?
- Who is my customer?
- Why will they pay?
- What alternatives exist?
- What is my edge?
- What is my unfair advantage?
- What is the simplest Minimum Viable Product (MVP)?

Most ideas you thought were "million dollar" will die at the canvas stage and that's good. Better for ideas to die than for you to die with them.

**Step 3: Build community before product.**

You don't need investors.

You don't need ads.

You don't need an office.

You need **people who care about your idea**.

Build:

- A small Instagram page
- A simple landing page
- A WhatsApp community
- A Telegram group

- A basic MVP
- A survey

Talk to people following similar brands.

Ask them what they need.

Ask what they hate.

Ask what they wish existed.

This is market research, not guesswork.

**Step 4: Launch ugly.**

Your first version will be bad.

Great.

Launch it anyway.

Every good business grows from imperfect birth.

Feedback > Perfection.

**Step 5: Use accelerators, not ego.**

If you're non-tech, find a technical co-founder.

Not someone who resonates with your vibe, but someone who resonates with your discipline.

If you're tech, find a business co-founder.

Someone who understands markets, storytelling, distribution.

There are plenty of accelerators in India (IIM incubators, NSRCEL, Startup India, VC bootcamps) that will help you build your structure.

**Step 6: Leave only when revenue matches your take-home.**

This is the final test.

When your startup generates:

- Your monthly take-home **OR**
- Your survival expenses (without fear)

Only then should you quit fully.

Entrepreneurship demands both heart and brain.

Emotion without logic is delusion.

Logic without courage is paralysis.

You need both.

And in the end, you only have two choices:

**Become bitter or become better.**

*But like Bhishma Pitamaha, your loyalty must never be to any kingdom, any king, any company, or any manager.*

*Your loyalty must be to your* ***Dharma:*** *your skill, your craft, your evolution.*

You are not bound to any organisation for life, even if they betray you.

You are only bound to your purpose.

And once you understand that, no toxic workplace can break you again.

# Chapter 7: Untapped Potential Under the Veil, In Vain

As I chewed on my slightly burnt tofu stir-fry and brown rice during a regular lunch break, my colleagues were busy being themselves. One of the self-proclaimed sigma males was rambling about the benefits of breastfeeding. Another was complaining about how his wife, also a working woman, no longer cooked for him. A third thought it perfectly acceptable to glance down my top because, in his words, "Why else do women come to workplaces? They're asking for it."

My mind wandered.

Despite my company offering an exceptional salary, there were very few women around. Even fewer in managerial roles. And in AI and data? As a strategic consultant or product manager, women were practically non-existent.

This puzzled me. Almost every woman I know carries a fire in her eyes. Whether she has chosen to be a homemaker, is pursuing her education, working full-time, taking a break, or surviving rural India through farming and animal rearing, there has never been a woman I've met who is content with not being involved in decision-making, not being treated with respect, or not earning her own money.

So what about women who are forced by family or societal norms to become homemakers against their will? Or women who "choose" it to keep the peace? Or women who juggle both?

Regardless of what a woman does or does not do, the numbers tell a brutal story.

According to the **Consumer Pyramids Household Survey (CPHS)** by the Centre for Monitoring Indian Economy (CMIE), covering individuals aged 15 and above from September 2019 to March 2023, women who are not part of the labour force spend over **7 hours daily** on unpaid household work. Even employed women spend **5.8 hours** daily. In contrast, men contribute significantly less, under **4 hours** per day if unemployed and **2.7 hours** if employed [22].

We talk about women losing ambition in 2026. As an extremely ambitious woman, I want to admit something honestly: I cannot do what I do without my house help or my mother. If I tried managing groceries, cooking, cleaning, and running errands alone, I would either burn out, fall sick, or miss out on work.

Because in tech, there is no concept of logging out, only sleeping. And even that gets shortened depending on the stakes you hold. 12 hours is a given, normal working shift for anyone in India! Period.

I often say to my mother, "How am I supposed to work, go to the gym, manage a home, and compete with men who have wives and mothers helping them? And on top of this, if I'm expected to get married and do the same work for two people, or worse, have a child, I will be nowhere in this race."

She smiled and replied, **"Looks like you don't want to be a wife. You need one."**

She was right.

### The Untapped Potential of Unpaid Labour

The untapped potential hidden in the unpaid labour women perform in India could contribute **24–32.4% of our GDP**. If we calculate the gross opportunity cost women lose by not taking up full-time employment or the cost of replacing their labour the estimated value of unpaid work in India ranges between ₹45,000 billion – ₹65,000 billion [22].

If women know they don't want this, and if we know as a country that we benefit not just by educating women but by employing them, then why don't we do it?

We call it *tradition.*

*Indian values.*

*Culture.*

"Women from respectable households don't work outside."

"Why should she work when her husband earns?"

Let's examine this more closely.

A country has income classes Destitute, Aspirer, Middle Class, Rich, and Affluent based on taxable income, but these categories only include earning members of a household. Women and children are often listed as dependents. But if you look closely, even in aspirer, middle, and rich households, women are often no more empowered than in destitute ones.

Spending power, purchasing decisions, investment control, and financial authority, even in 2026, are largely held by male members of the family.

Women lack agency not because they lack ambition, but because they lack structural support. In large parts of rural India, this is due to lack of formal education. In urban India, it manifests as a lack of employable skills despite having degrees. This pattern is also visible in countries like Iran, Egypt, and Jordan.

The most effective intervention globally has been **investment in Early Childhood Care and Education (ECCE).** In countries like Sweden and Bulgaria, less than 10% of women stay out of the labour force to care for children and households [22].

### Talent Buried Inside Four Walls

Growing up, my mother was exceptionally talented in mathematics. So much so that until the 10th grade, I didn't need a tutor and I eventually went on to earn an MSc in Data Science. Genetics helped, sure, and my father's investment in education mattered, but her brilliance was undeniable.

Yet at every PTA meeting, when she saw other mothers who were employed, financially independent, and socially confident, she felt embarrassed. Not because she wasn't capable but because she wasn't allowed.

Many such talented women suffocate their intelligence and abilities within four walls because culturally, men are expected to go out and "hunt," while women are expected to hold the fort.

In foreign universities, students from some of the wealthiest households across the globe are required to divide chores equally. Everyone is taught to master at least one household task. Failure means collective punishment. These institutions are subtly teaching both genders dignity of labour and domestic competence. This experience humbles you!

So why do Indian men contribute less than three hours a day to household work?

They are not busy changing the world or launching Mars rovers. They are watching IPL, playing video games, or consuming porn in hostel rooms.

We encourage men to loiter, explore hobbies, and take up space, while women are confined indoors in the name of safety and honour. This pattern repeats, resulting in fewer women monetising their talents and more women sitting at home, labelled "respectable."

My father once tried to encourage my mother to pursue education and work even after marriage. The community shamed him:

"Mr. Reddy, you're making your woman work now?"

Today, both my sister and I are employed in top companies, holding postgraduate degrees from foreign universities. Perhaps that hunger was subconsciously passed down from witnessing the wasted potential of a brilliant woman in our bloodline.

As first-generation professionals from a traditional Indian family, we understand the kind of empowerment a woman gains through employment, even within a family. The power to walk out of abusive marriages, to leave situations with grace instead of begging for dignity, and to say "*no*" as a full sentence.

Employment, financial independence, and respect earned beyond one's surname purely through ability, conduct, and command over one's craft, money, and body translate very differently.

**Unpaid, Thankless Labour**

As of October 2025, the average monthly salary of a full-time domestic worker in Bangalore, Mumbai, or Delhi ranges between **₹20,000 – ₹25,000**. Some families even prefer live-in help from Tier 1 or Tier 2 cities, offering food, shelter, and minimal allowance. These workers often secure better education for their children and employment for their spouses as drivers in the same households.

This system works because it benefits the aspirer class roughly 50% of the population earning between ₹20,000 and ₹30,000 per month. Simultaneously, the middle class and the top 10% depend heavily on domestic labour to build careers that ultimately fuel the top 1% and their companies [8].

But this system comes at a cost.

A large portion of both the aspirer and middle classes is sustained by unpaid labour, most often by wives and mothers, sometimes daughters, whose contributions are confined to caregiving and domestic work, with little opportunity or encouragement to explore identity or purpose beyond the home.

This results in limited worldviews, emotionally dysregulated family dynamics, suppressed sexuality, unaddressed trauma, unsafe pregnancies, exhausting childbirth, overwhelming child-rearing responsibilities, and most importantly, complete loss of identity without being paid even a single rupee for the trade-off.

These women are the real soft power behind India's economic engine. They clean, cook, emotionally regulate, sexually service, and feed employees so they can work 12-hour days, six days a week, while being paid for eight hours across five days. In service contracts, Indian labour is billed to foreign clients in thousands of dollars per hour, while workers receive only tens of dollars.

Startups in San Francisco boast of cheap labour, efficient AI talent, and flexible work cultures fuelled by Indian workers whose productivity is sustained by invisible, unpaid women.

When people migrate abroad to "build careers," they often escape only the optics, not the structure. Homemakers in India become homemakers abroad. Cleaner air, better infrastructure, improved dating prospects but the same gender roles.

**Controlled Independence**

India offers women controlled independence, enough to benefit society, but not enough to liberate themselves.

Work-from-home has worsened this. Women now earn from home, manage domestic labour, raise children, and lose their right to socialise all under one roof. This lifestyle allows them to stay on the good side of family, landlords, banks, workplaces, and the capitalist framework.

If society were truly accepting of single women, ask yourself how many marriages would actually survive?

Patriarchal capitalist societies do not want women empowered. Who else would tolerate entitlement, provide unpaid support, and reproduce the next workforce?

This exhaustion of "good girl" conditioning suppresses women, leaving them unhappy and resentful. That resentment then spills onto soft targets—female colleagues, friends, daughters-in-law, mothers-in-law, sisters—all destroying sisterhood.

From my interactions with women across cultures of India, Iran, China, Morocco, the UK, the US, France, I have noticed that in economically constrained, male-centric societies, women are more likely to sabotage other women. Carried-over anger and disapproval from their own lives are projected onto those closest to them.

A happy mind seeks collaboration and growth. An oppressed one seeks control.

If women were genuinely happy, encouraged, and empowered, how would capitalism benefit?

**Luxury of Choice**

When will women truly hold their truth and uphold it. This whole "get married before 25, have children before 30, retire at 35" mission statement for women is outdated! I know there is still a small society of women who are the outliers of this demographic, but that must change faster!

Intelligent, morally strong women who choose to step out of this systematic madness, are termed difficult, guilt tripped and isolated, as this society has no idea how to receive the truly liberated feminine.

Below are some of the observations I have made based on my interactions with both women who chose to be homemakers and lead meaningful and fulfilling families, people who have been forced into it, and people who have chosen to escape the matrix (like me). **We could help people make more gender balanced choices by:**

1. Creating a systematic shift in the lifestyle of young girls right from their early-childhood, enabling them to pick sports, play in the sun, and fight their battles from a young age instead of locking them up in the homes under the pretext of protecting them or their "chastity".
2. Replicating what Sweden has done; attempted to create playgrounds that can accommodate young girls, who will not have to fight the male gaze, and can bond over football instead of house-house. We can teach girls it's okay to play in the sun and get tanned; that their fair skin will do them more harm than the tan, both in protecting them from cancer and cancerian men!
3. Empowering women to develop employable skills which they can monetise, rather than glorified university degrees which may or may not enable them in their livelihoods.
4. Normalise walking away from toxic marriages and relationships as a society, not just on social media but in real life.
5. Making girls focus on building their personalities before a crisis arises. By picking meaningful friendships

as opposed to compulsive groups of friends who don't evolve or let you evolve. Pick people who are self-disciplined and have clarity in goals.

6. As a gender, refrain from seeking validation or asking permission to lead our lives. Yes, *beti padhao, but no beti badhao.* Nobody wants you to excel beyond control, they want you to be just about independent so you are not a liability, but not so much that you are an autonomously thinking asset who serves her own person.
7. Not falling for the you-are-pretty-you-will-find-a-great-husband trope! If God made you distinctly beautiful, then he wants you to spend time less in front of the mirror and more in front of the world, changing the face of your genome, your species. Yes, beautiful people get heard, but smart, hardworking people get taken seriously.
8. Lastly, as women, we need to practice the audacity and confidence that absolutely mediocre men possess. Confidence is the most underrated quality that can flip any narrative. No matter your status quo, keep your chin up!

# Chapter 8: Only 4% Women on Top?

If you believe that men and women stand on equal ground in the tech world, especially in India, then this chapter will feel like fiction to you. But for the rest of us—the majority—it is not fiction. It is a lived truth. The untapped potential of the brilliant woman in tech who succumbs to isolation on a day-to-day basis due to the bro code culture at work is shocking. The way women are discouraged from focusing on their core skill and instead made to focus on whether their lipstick is provocative or their skirt length is too distracting. Women still don't believe trainings like POSH or Inclusive Awareness move the needle in our favour.

## Pretty Privilege is Pretty Punishment

Women are hired with all the intent to promote or improve gender ratios in teams, but why are companies failing to retain them? Be it the labels of diversity hires or the comments of "whom did she sleep with to get here," women are always judged and hate-mongered—especially as tech leaders. In a country that throngs Durga poojas and Dussehra processions, why is it so hard to just see your female leader for her worth and not what lies between her legs? It is astonishing to see the direly small percentage of women in cutting-edge tech, often in single-digit percentages, leave alone women rising to become AI or data leaders (from an Indian heritage).

In India today, 40% of women who enter tech leave within the first 5-8 years [13] [12]. That statistic is not a number. It is a cemetery. It is the graveyard of thousands of ambitions, exam ranks, coding bootcamps, education loans, and dreams that were once alive, breathing, and hopeful. These women begin their careers with the same enthusiasm, the same hunger, the same glossy onboarding photos as their male peers. And then something happens: not one big blow, but a series of small, relentless chisels. Family pressure. Marriage pressure. The subtle noose of "settle down." The whispered warnings that "career is fine, but don't forget your real duties."

Even in 2025, with remote work becoming the new norm in India, with house-help support in every metro city, with hybrid work policies, with laptop lifestyles and co-working spaces—20% of women still drop out before touching mid-senior roles. The system doesn't push them out with one shove. It erodes them grain by grain.

It is the same erosion that sands the faces on old temple walls: slow, silent, inevitable [13].

Women are expected to become the primary caregivers, no matter the size of their paycheck. Their income is welcomed. Their autonomy is negotiable. Any assertive behaviour from women is easily dismissed with comments like, "She needs to get some," or "Is she PMSing?" But male counterparts being assertive is seen as a sign of holding the team accountable and being a leader who gives a damn.

And so, when a woman decides she wants both a life and a career, she becomes an anomaly. An irritation. A rebellion. A question mark in a system that only understands full stops.

### The Illusion of Inclusion

Corporate India loves its diversity posters. Loves its panel discussions. Loves the token women in the front row with perfectly ironed shirts and forced smiles. But here is the secret nobody says aloud: many diversity hires are made to fill a quota, not a gap. When I was hired as the tech product leader of an all-boys camp, while many colleagues mocked me as a diversity hire, in reality the team had spent 4 months and lakhs of Indian rupees to fill the position, hire, and train me.

Behind the scenes, the employees who fought tooth and nail to climb the corporate ladder look at the woman hired beside them and feel... replaced. Threatened. Resentful. They assume the system has handed her an opportunity with a pink ribbon simply because she is a woman.

If that woman is hired laterally, at a leadership level, the resentment deepens. "She skipped the line," they think. "She hasn't suffered what we suffered." "She probably is a diversity hire." "Wonder whom she had to bed to get that far, that soon."

The irony is delicious and tragic. Because women suffer more—just differently, silently, without recognition or reward.

But this resentment isn't only Indian, it's global. A legacy of Victorian morality exported by colonial machinery. A worldview where women are meant to nurture, not lead.

How period leave bills passed by the Government of Karnataka or the Government of Telangana in India enabling more flexible work-from-home options for women are all seen as special treatment by majority at work—honestly, these are half of the problem. The fact that we can't participate in randy male joke-based bonding where most important decisions are made amidst sexist comments on their wives, female colleagues, and Bollywood actresses, limits our chance to participate in the decision-making process

Culturally, we don't make it easy for women to belong in positions of power and own it. We push them to become hyper-vigilant, extremely aggressive, and defensive, at the expense of distracting them from their main purpose.

So much untapped potential lost in protecting the ego of male counterparts! If we want better productivity at work like Narayana Murthy sir proposes—9 a.m. to 9 p.m. work hours for six days a week—avoid gatekeeping technical knowledge and job roles so women can participate equally.

Give women positions of power and let them enable and empower other women. We need to grow as individuals in order for companies to grow, and eventually, countries to grow.

And yet, long before colonisers, India had women kings, women warriors, women philosophers. This country was not unfamiliar with female leadership. It is colonial residue that made the idea “unnatural.”

Today, that residue still stains corporate conference rooms.

**The Interview Interrogation**

Every woman in tech knows the script.

A job interview for her includes the following detours:

“Are you planning to get married soon?”

“Are you planning to have a baby anytime soon?”

“Who will take care of them?”

“Does your husband support your working late?”

“Do you have family obligations to prevent you from working late hours?”

These questions are coded landmines. Career suicide disguised as “casual conversation.” And the irony? If she calls this out, she becomes the problem.

Change will not happen through personal protest.

It has to come from systemic correction, led by powerful men and women who understand the rot beneath the polished office floors.

One of my first interviews in a Bangalore-based MNC soon after my graduation was with a VP of a health-tech company, who wasted his time and mine by dismissively asking why I needed the job when I came from a good family background. Somehow, in the south of India, my surname beckons unwanted stigma around coming from wealth. He spent a good one hour of his time, and two hours of my commute time on the way from Silk Board to Manyata Tech Park in peak traffic, only to insult me for being fair, attractive, and studying in a Bangalore-based women's college—where he felt women only do drugs or have sex with anything that walks. After which, he didn't even have the courtesy to swipe me out and left me waiting for the security guard to get me, after 15 minutes of waiting post the interview.

This exposure led me to pursue my master's without attending further interviews. I am pretty sure today this wasn't an isolated incident. Men in leadership roles—some of them—do judge and deem young, ambitious women to be desperate. They feel obligated to disrespect and "show them their place."

This behaviour is gladly encouraged, as it makes it easier to gatekeep good roles, powerful decision-making boardrooms, knowledge, and ultimately the wealth associated with it.

## Open Blind Spots Nobody Wants to Address

Now comes the demon nobody wants to look in the eye: sexual advances at work.

This demon takes many forms—subtle comments, inappropriate jokes, late-night messages, forced proximity, or outright propositions. Every woman, and I say this with full responsibility, every second woman in tech has encountered something inappropriate—whether verbal, physical, or emotional.

And when she speaks?

She gets drowned in a sea of advice:

"Why didn't you avoid him?"

"What were you wearing?"

"Maybe he didn't mean it like that."

"Are you exaggerating?"

"Just ignore it."

Even worse, some women—indoctrinated by patriarchy—become foot soldiers in protecting the system. Their words cut deeper than men's, because betrayal by your own gender is a wound that doesn't close.

When a woman rejects an inappropriate advance, the man doesn't always retreat. Sometimes he retaliates. The professional battlefield becomes personal. Every meeting becomes a war. Every deliverable is doubted. Every hallway conversation carries a hidden jab.

She bleeds emotionally until she either becomes numb, leaves the job, leaves the company, or leaves the industry altogether—in my case, the country, as my work visa depended on the company's willingness to sponsor it.

**The Gossip Economy of Tech**

I wish I could say the Indian tech world runs on intelligence and innovation. But let me speak the truth most HR teams bury under their carpets: tech runs on gossip. On chai-time rumours. On WhatsApp groups. On sexualising women. On judging their clothes, relationships, breakups, makeup, weight, and confidence.

This is how alliances form.

This is how "team bonding" happens.

This is how men build their networks.

The same men who lord over their wives at home cannot stand the idea of taking instructions from a woman manager. Their egos are too fragile, too entitled, too inherited.

Worse are the **brainwashed agents of patriarchy**—most of the time women by gender, but with a mindset that is completely **self-discriminatory**.

For some reason, they have normalised a **submissive, subservient version of our gender**, one that makes everyone with a misogynistic mindset deeply comfortable.

Anyone who doesn't adhere to this script—who opposes it or even slightly questions why this **second-class-citizen treatment** is normalised—is severely mocked, isolated, and potentially rendered an **outcast**.

## The Cost of Being a Woman in Tech

When a woman faces stonewalling, silencing, questioning humiliation, isolation, gossip, disrespect, emotional labour, double standards, and pay disparity, **what happens?**

She returns home emotionally drained, and the chaos spills into her domestic life. Eventually she quits—not because she lacked ambition, but because the system lacked humanity.

Indian women are given the "good girl" conditioning right from childhood:

- not to talk back
- not to challenge
- not to assert
- not to say "no"
- not to put themselves first

You cannot suddenly expect her to practise boundaries in the office when she was denied permission to practise them at home.

**So, What Can Be Done?**

This isn't a "women in tech" poster problem.

This is a cultural rehabilitation problem:

**1. A Community for Women, by Women**

Women in technical roles rarely have the luxury of friendship outside work.

They need spaces where:

- Nobody is evaluating them
- Nobody is sexualising them
- Nobody is competing with them
- Nobody is judging their womanhood or ambition

Just a safe, sacred community.

Not just book clubs. Not just weekend brunches. Not just fitness groups. Not just walk-and-talk circles or peer mentoring.

A space that normalises women being **fiercely ambitious**—owning it, talking about it openly, and being applauded for it. Because **womanhood and ambition are not mutually exclusive.**

This is how self-esteem gets rebuilt—**in the presence of other women.**

**2. Mindset over Skillset**

We need **pace-makers and trailblazers** not only in technology or EBITDA.

We need **progressive, excellent human beings** in organisations—leaders who enable women and diversity to thrive and who become true agents of change.

These are the men and women who are not brainwashed by patriarchy, nor afraid to provide equal opportunity, **without compromising on deliverables or outcomes**.

They must become a force of influence, rewrite management textbooks, and be held as the **gold standard of leadership**.

These are the kinds of leaders we should celebrate as the *Forbes 40 Under 40*—people who lead with **grace, responsibility, and inclusivity**.

These should be the parameters by which we **gauge the leaders of tomorrow**.

3. **Empower Middle Management to "Company Culture" Ambassadors**

Middle managers know exactly how the sewage of corporate behaviour flows.

Give them the power to:

- Translate the company's visionary culture into action.
- Be a whistle-blower without losing out on opportunities.
- Block harassment even if its passive or indirect.
- Regulate behaviour when concerns are raised.
- Uplift talent and empower other female colleagues.

Because ultimately, culture grows bottom-up, not top-down.

**Gender Disparity Is Not History—It Is Today**

*Remember how Draupadi had no participation in the game of dice between the cunning Kauravas and the naïve Pandavas, yet she bore the bloodiest consequences of that game.* It is eerily synonymous with corporate culture today, where women are excluded and undermined in critical strategic decisions, yet never spared from their consequences.

We cannot talk our way out of misogyny.

We cannot hashtag our way out of sexism.

We cannot workshop our way out of patriarchal conditioning.

Women do not need tokenism.

Women need systems, structures, cultures, and communities that allow them to exist fully: as individuals, professionals, and human beings.

We were never meant to survive this male-dominated world.

But we will.

And we will change it, **one department, one decision, one woman at a time!**

# Chapter 9: When in Doubt, Always Stick to Your Values

After these two disastrous stints as a product manager, with a London studio apartment rent to pay, a Russell Group university MSc Data Science degree student loan owed to the Punjab National Bank (think Vijay Mallya's airlines debt, jinxed bank I tell you), I was under immediate and immense pressure to find another job. So, I went on LinkedIn and updated my profile to "open to work." Whilst on garden leave, I started making applications but the loneliness of not having my products to manage, my team to interact with, my colleagues to banter with—it all hit me like cocaine withdrawal.

I hadn't met a lot of people as passionate about their craft as me; some people even call me obsessive, but I wake up every day genuinely excited to be able to produce the kind of AI products I can, which not only is flex and hobby, it also pays my bills. I really enjoy doing what I do for a living, so not having that without my choice put me in depression of sorts.

## Some Rules are Meant to be Broken

At this point since I was on garden leave, I couldn't talk to anyone except a good friend, who was also my coworker. He would visit me regardless of the hassle at work, fully knowing he was risking his own job. He was Caucasian by race but almost Asian at heart, so our rapport was comforting; he was so loyal, kind, and chivalrous, it almost made me forget my pain when I was around him. Although, I don't endorse workplace romance, he was a six-foot-three-inch tall Caucasian man in spectacles, who explained crypto during our lunch dates, solved my data issues at work and accompanied me on my short weekend hikes while we chatted about quantum physics—I mean this guy was a dream. I couldn't fight the fact that we were colleagues, a girl can only dodge so many bullets! This relationship for me was an eye opener, given most patriarchal societies don't incentivise equal relationship dynamics, this kind of treatment has set the bar too high.

This experience healed the scars he never caused, so when life gives you pain, it also finds you the right people to heal it as well. Though against my values to never shit where you eat, this was one of those blurred-line rules I am glad I broke. When we broke up for personal reasons, he requested if we can remain friends after the break up; I did try to blur another of my lines for him, but it never worked. I was too jealous to watch him move on. I couldn't have a toxic friendship; I would rather have a healthy break up. He hated it at that moment and still does. I still can't erase the expression on his face, flushed and almost teary, when we met for the last time. I didn't announce that I was leaving for India at that time or that our break up was final. It was just one of those energy-vibration things where he knew, I knew, we knew that this was the end of something beautiful. As if the sun was setting on something, as if we would never be in each other's gazes, each other's arms, or in each other's minds ever again. I am not a big endorser of love either, but I do know that you don't just have one in a lifetime. You have multiple, and whatever he and I had was so precious that it was nothing less or nothing more than love. At this point we are discussing values, so it is pretty much subjective and situational; sometimes being too rigid makes you lose out on the best moments of your life, sometimes being too kind puts you in situations you were better off without.

**So, knowing when to ride the tide and when to avoid it is the real deal.**

Well, regardless, I always believe in following my instincts, and it has worked brilliantly in my favour.

## Final Stint in the UK

Amidst all this, I was aimlessly making applications for the third time, fourth actually, but we will get there eventually. I also ended up making a few applications to incubators in the UK, based on my previous entrepreneurial experience (which we will get to later). To my surprise, after all these efforts, I got a LinkedIn message from my nemesis from university, whom I never liked for reasons we will introspect later. The nemesis offered me a role in the company he was employed at, but one that wasn't really well-established in the UK.

The role, when introduced to me, was hybrid, but once I joined, I realised it was completely remote. Well, anyway, there were many loopholes not only in the recruitment process, the HR policies, and the conduct of the interviewers, but also in the culture of the company, which was fucked up. This was established from day zero, but now that I was exhausted from nitpicking, running from pillar to post, and yet I seemed to have not learnt my final lesson, so I said a tentative yes. I was still struggling to choose what was best for me, but was willing to pick the easiest available route. Well, the burnout, both emotional and intellectual, was real at this point.

After a bumpy start I began work. Before joining I even took a couple days off to quickly visit my folks back in India; this is when I got acceptance into an incubator in Cambridge.

Again, decision-making has to be done clearly; this is one of the hardest lessons I have learnt so far. I accepted both the offers, the one that paid my rent and the one that could potentially help me buy the street, not knowing that sometimes you can't have it all, especially when you have high stakes such as visa sponsorship.

I ended up juggling both, but my primary employer had a problem with this level of ambition.

I was paid a salary that month, but I wasn't deployed to any project and was on the bench; my reporting manager was on his annual leave. With all these ongoing issues and my urge to work on my startup dream, I again took a decision to quit this job within a month of joining. But this decision was more a result of the constant tug of war between HR being unhelpful, my manager being a good cop, and my friend who hired me stonewalling me with crucial product-related information (incidentally, since it was a very small company, he was my lead engineer too).

**No Such Thing as Bad Decisions**

With so much going on, I was too confused to decode the situation. I also had two horrible nights at Cambridge, juggling in-person meetings in Central London and networking events at Cambridge. At this point, my mental health was giving way, and even small inconveniences appeared ghastly to me. It was the onset of the British winter, which led to the seasonal depression, along with my ongoing undiagnosed thyroid and fatty liver conditions, an added body fat percentage, a decline in confidence, and PTSD from past jobs.

I decided to quit everything and dropped a notice to my landlord, which turned into another mind fuck, where the real estate agents and landlords in London scam immigrants out of money during untimely end of contracts. They started threatening me with legal action if I didn't pay up for the early exit. Given my mental health was always quite horrible, at this point I was feeling like everything was working against me. Though **this last company** was full of Indians in India and just my wannabe university nemesis was in the UK (everyone else was literally Indians and in India), I somehow got fed up with the UK, blamed it for these problems, and decided to head back to the problem source.

**Weirdest decision** of my life. I don't know what values I was trying to stick to at this point; it looks like a complete

**flight response** to these problems. I don't even think I gave it a thought before making such a big decision; something at this point had saturated within me. I still had a good seven months on my Post-Study Work Visa and I could have made it. But I decided to head home.

I still had some chance to resolve the issues at this new workplace, but the toxic culture, as I witnessed, was heavily influenced by two things:

1. Onsite folks being superior and bullish towards onshore folks.
2. Hierarchy being enforced to get work done as opposed to process enforcement.
3. Unilateral Unidirectional conversations, ego-driven leadership, and hero-centric approach to daily work as opposed to innovation-centric, collaborative, and conversational approach.
4. My manager, the CTO, was a textbook example of narcissistic leadership. Which meant, everything he said and did was right, and the rest of us were to, "yes boss" around him.

## Value Your Values

My whole value system asked me just one question: how do you want to make your bread? How do you want to sleep at night? How do you want to be after 5 years? Like this guy? Because we don't realise this—whom we work with, how we make our bread, what thoughts we let into our minds during our waking and sleeping hours significantly change us. You only notice this once it's too late. For me, the whole point was the "why". The "why" of my moving to the UK. It was to build a career in AI and settle there for a better quality of life. I am sure somewhere down the lane I would have done both of these even in these toxic workplaces, but would I still be the same me to enjoy what I built?

I would risk losing the very empathy, the human-centric, optimistic, innovative, energetic personality of mine in the means of gaining everything else. That, to me, was way more priceless than everything else that had seemed luring at the moment—it still does. The alleys of South Bank, St Paul's Cathedral, the food courts in Piccadilly, the stores of Old Bond Street, the lifestyle I had in my West London apartment were all too smooth to lose. But when it stood against losing my innate nature, I think it was a no-brainer for me. Given my bad mental state, I couldn't figure out why I took these decisions; they seemed reckless to my parents. To me, it didn't seem like one shocker after another. I was also too disappointed, defeated, emotionally burnt out to figure these things out. On top of moving back into my toxic household where everything came crashing down, from me wasting money by moving abroad.

**Dire Consequences**

I had to immediately start finding a way to fend for myself, as the only remaining savings I had were invested in the stock market, which crashed at the end of December 2024. At this point, I was surprised as to why I even tried to do anything at all, but that's human nature, to relentlessly try despite the risk of failure, suffering, and hurt. This human spirit of sheer courage is what distinguishes us from the rest of the ecosystem, the human spirit of survival, especially when money, or lack of it, is involved. Yet, how do values always win even in the face of morals? Perhaps that's why I feel well at night, enjoy my meals, and live a guilt-free life.

**Remember, there are no free lunches; if it's free, then you are probably on the menu!**

# Chapter 10: Death by Overwork

I stood at Tower Bridge one icy London evening, fingers stiff inside cheap faux-leather gloves, breath fogging into a mist that made the whole city look like an old British postcard. The Thames below moved with that cold, imperial indifference only ancient rivers possess—gliding as if it carried not water but centuries of power, conquest, sin, tea, blood, and human exhaustion.

And for one long, sharp, terrifying moment, I wondered:

**If I jumped, would they convict me for attempted suicide?**

Or if I died:

**Would I finally earn a moment of silence?**

People love to talk about "hitting rock bottom" as if it's a cinematic thud—one neat crash, followed by a redemption montage. But rock bottom is never one moment. It's granular. It has layers, sediments, fossils of dead dreams. I wasn't at the bottom. I was a thousand feet beneath it, drifting somewhere in the trenches of my own psyche.

In my mind, I saw myself diving.

The cold, black water slapping me into non-existence.

Then—suddenly—the cosmic projector switched on.

My entire life unspooled in a frantic montage:

My birth.

My first love.

My first pet.

My first heartbreak.

The first time my parents tried to discipline me with hands instead of reasoning.

My first paycheck.

My first betrayal.

Everything flashed in a kaleidoscope, like a reel the universe had been saving for a dramatic moment.

As I sank deeper in the Thames River, it felt like I was sinking into a deeper state of imagination, dream, astral projection, or spiritual delirium; I don't know—I fell into what felt like a vortex. Not the clichéd tunnel with a white light and angels waiting. No, this was a karmic cyclone. A spinning, violent, all-revealing spiral.

Inside it were **a thousand versions of my life**.

Same souls.

Same lessons.

Different costumes.

Different outcomes.

Love in one life.

Betrayal in another.

Lust in another.

Compassion in one.

Cruelty in the next.

*It was the Mahabharata refracted across lifetimes—Karna's loyalty, Draupadi's rage, Arjuna's confusion, Bhishma's oath, Shakuni's cunning, all combined into a cosmic pattern I was doomed to repeat until I learned the damn lesson.*

And in that swirling metaphysical mess, something struck me:

**Death is not the answer.**

There is no divine exit exam.

No god at the door saying, "You may leave now, *beta*."

No loophole to escape the spiral.

If I died, the vortex would simply spit me out into another existence—maybe as a fish, a squirrel, a lone wolf, an ant, or, knowing my luck, a bloody laptop charger—destined to complete the same karmic homework in a different form.

My mission here wasn't complete.

My spiral hadn't run its course.

And then betrayal of betrayals: my alarm rang.

**BRRRT BRRRT: 7:45 a.m., London**

A calendar invite flashed:

**"Ad-hoc 1:1 with Manager—9:00 a.m."**

If there is a sound that can force a soul back into a broken body faster than divine intervention, it is the ping of a meeting invite.

### The Immigrant Chakravyuha

There is a special kind of anxiety reserved for immigrant employees. People assume losing your job means losing income. Cute. Try again.

Losing your job abroad means losing:

- your visa
- your right to stay

- your house
- your stability
- your painstakingly built life
- your identity
- your illusion of belonging

It is not *just* a job.

It is the thread holding your entire existence together.

My manager knew this.

And like all mediocre men threatened by a competent woman, he weaponised it.

"I just want to give you some constructive feedback," he would say, with that fake-soft British corporate tone. But every word was a landmine dressed in politeness. Psychological warfare with a smile.

Every meeting with him felt like Abhimanyu entering the Chakravyuha—trained only to enter, not to come out alive.

**Gaslighting as a Management Skill**

In the corporate interrogation room, sorry, meeting room, he leaned back like he owned the Thames and began his performance.

"You haven't put in enough effort."

"You need to improve communication."

"The client feels your written documentation is lacking."

Funny, because in the one year I spent breaking my back for that company:

- I launched **two** major products end-to-end.

- Juggled **IST, EST, PST** time zones like a circus act.
- Pulled all-nighters data modelling and solutioning with engineers.
- Travelled London → Vegas → London for requirement-gathering sessions.
- Knew the product better than the engineers who built it.

But apparently, my communication wasn't "up to the mark."

Ah yes, the favourite line of managers preparing your funeral.

Then came the blow:

**"I'm putting you on a Performance Improvement Plan."**

For what?

Because I refused to be demoted from Product Manager to Business Analyst, the corporate equivalent of being told:

"Sit quietly in the corner while we steal your work."

The biggest red flag?

All Jira tickets suddenly reassigned from my name to his overnight, as if erasing my contributions would make him look competent in the restructuring.

It wasn't my fault.

It wasn't my performance.

It wasn't my "communication."

It was his fear.

He needed my role to survive.

So he chose the oldest corporate trick:

**Discredit the woman who threatens you.**

### Then Came the Creepy Senior Manager

If my manager was the serpent, his boss was the hungry python.

He requested a "private chat" after hours, the kind of email that makes every woman's spine stiffen.

The meeting was not in the office.

It was at a dimly-lit pub in West London.

What was supposed to be a discussion turned into a proposition delivered with the grace of a drunk bull.

He hinted that my:

- visa
- job
- career progression
- opportunities
- future

...could all be secured, *if* I considered "getting to know him better."

Every personal detail I had reluctantly shared in my one-on-one meetings had been carried like gossip to this man.

He wanted companionship.

I wanted dignity.

I looked at him, venmoed £20 for the dinner, said, "You can expect my resignation tomorrow morning."

He choked on his burger.

I walked out into the cold Chiswick night like a woman who had burned her last bridge but saved her soul.

He followed me to the bus stop for one final attempt.

I said, "No," with the precision of a guillotine.

And that was that.

## The Price of Choosing Yourself

People assume quitting is brave.

It is not.

It is terrifying.

It is lonely.

It is expensive.

Leaving cost me:

- months of unemployment
- spiralling self-doubt
- relocation trauma
- loss of my London life
- the abrupt death of friendships
- the fog of depression
- and the dread of starting over

And India welcomed me back with ancestral property disputes, the kind that make you question genetics, lineage, and the point of civilisation.

The cultural whiplash was real:

West London tennis courts → Bangalore traffic

Tube rides → auto rides

Pret → pani puri

Chiswick pubs → HSR breweries

My body was here.

My soul lagged somewhere over the Arabian Sea.

But rock bottom, as I said, is soil.

And soil grows things.

**The Rebirth in Bangalore**

A few months into the emotional rubble, the job market opened its reluctant doors. I interviewed with the exhaustion of a woman who had been burned but still carried fire.

And then one afternoon—no epiphany, no cosmic sign, just a simple email—came an offer.

A real one.

A good one.

A **better** one.

A role in Bangalore:

- higher package
- better title
- a respectful team
- a humane culture
- actual career progression
- no visa leash around my neck

The irony wasn't lost on me.

I crossed continents searching for dignity and found it in the city I had once vowed never to return to.

I rebuilt slowly, like a temple after an earthquake.

Brick by brick.

Meeting by meeting.

Boundary by boundary.

And one afternoon, in the middle of a routine stand-up meeting, surrounded by engineers who respected my voice, I realised something:

I had survived.

And more importantly:

**I had resurrected.**

Not in the dramatic Bollywood way.

Not in a "flames to phoenix" montage.

But in the quiet, dignified way only women understand: the kind built from patience, rage alchemised into wisdom, and the refusal to bend to the fragile misogyny.

London broke a version of me.

Bangalore grew a new one.

Maybe reincarnation is not a next life.

Maybe it is the next version of ourselves—the one we become *after* we've died a few times within this one.

# Chapter 11:
# Why AI Won't Make Up for Poor Leadership

"Will I be replaced at work by AI?" is the loudest question of the past couple of years! Let's understand what AI is.

Artificial Intelligence is an umbrella term used to describe techniques and computer programmes that mimic aspects of human intelligence. The emphasis on the word "mimic" is critical. AI does not possess intelligence in the way humans do; it reproduces patterns of intelligence as they appear in data.

**AI Myth Buster!**

This distinction matters because even today, our understanding of human intelligence remains incomplete. Neuroscientists, evolutionary biologists, psychologists, and psychiatrists still debate its origins, structure, and limits. If human intelligence itself is not fully understood, the idea that we can replicate it so completely that humans become obsolete is, at best, speculative–and at worst, deeply misleading.

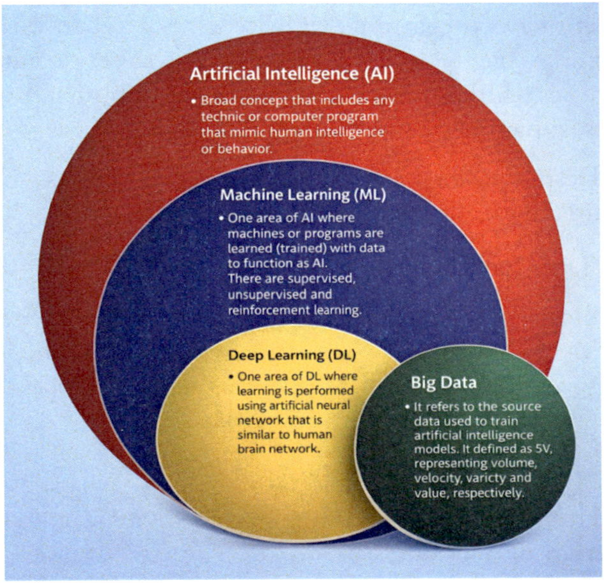


**Figure 1:** Graphical representation of AI and its derivative terms, along with the role of Big Data. Source: [18]

## From Machine Learning to Agents

Machine Learning refers to systems trained on data—large or small—to produce behaviour that appears intelligent. These systems may use supervised, unsupervised, semi-supervised, or reinforcement learning approaches. They do not think; they optimise.

Deep Learning extends this paradigm by using neural networks loosely inspired by biological neurons. While the metaphor is powerful, it remains just that—a metaphor. Artificial neural networks are mathematical constructs, not conscious entities.

Today, AI is often conflated with its derivatives: Generative AI and Agent-based AI. Generative AI is fundamentally a subset of Deep Learning, which itself is a subset of Machine Learning. Agent AI, on the other hand, focuses on automating processes through bots—sometimes with human validation loops, sometimes without.

Despite their differences, all these systems share one essential dependency: data.

## The Data Paradox

Most AI systems today are trained on data sourced from the open internet—Wikipedia, Reddit, YouTube, forums, blogs, and social platforms. But this raises a critical question: who created this data in the first place?

The answer is simple—humans.

Human curiosity. Human creativity. Human lived experience.

If we collectively stop exercising our own creativity and outsource thinking entirely to machines, then in a few years, AI will be training itself on recycled outputs—derivatives of derivatives. A closed loop of synthetic content. Signal diluted into noise.

**And beyond cognition lies an even greater challenge: empathy.** How does one replicate something as profoundly human as emotional understanding, moral intuition, or compassion born of suffering?

The last five years have seen an explosive rise in data and AI. But the need to evolve as humans is more important than ever.

People are panic-upskilling in GenAI and Data Science from any vendor offering a quick LinkedIn badge. There's this insane urgency to know *everything, now*. It's adding immense pressure on professionals.

Being good at your skillset is only half the battle won. You also need to understand AI basics and how they apply to your role. But after long hours of work, emotional labour, traffic, and recovery, who has time to even process their emotions?

Social media doesn't help either—it's amplifying everything to a point of information overload.

**Evolving as a Human**

Sounds like spiritual nirvana talk, but trust me, it's just about daily awareness.

I, for one, don't believe the IT pace even allows regular meditation.

So, here's a practical approach: focus on the *human* aspect of yourself—the one who ran barefoot as a kid, the one who endured heartbreaks and still found beauty, the one who will remain when the masks are off.

Connect with that self.

There's no greater compassion than **self-compassion.**

When you walk into your workplace, do you acknowledge the security guard? Smile or nod? Say good morning?

What about the Uber driver—do you start with a "hello," end with a "sir"?

Why is this important?

Because the 1–10% of us privileged enough to afford politeness actually set the tone.

How many of us notice the people cleaning our office? That's where mindfulness begins.

If you're not feeling human at work, and you think just finishing your tasks is enough—you're trapped in the capitalist delusion of productivity over presence.

## Bringing Humanity to Work

AI can't make up for lack of empathy–sometimes that might not be such a bad thing, to be honest.

Once, my colleague's tone, mood, and efficiency were off. I tried to enquire whether he was coping with issues outside of work or if work itself was causing stress. He revealed he was in therapy. From that day, his productivity doubled not because his problems vanished, but because he felt seen. He felt the human in him could show up to work.

There's a downside, of course. People can take advantage.

When I joined a new role, the team refused to discuss any product-related details with me. I tried everything possible like setting up processes, trying to mingle with the team, asking for knowledge transfer or inclusion in project planning. After six months, when I got tired and informed my immediate reporting manager, he said, "Well, you are only a product manager. You have not contributed technically in this team, so the team doesn't respect you. In order to earn their respect, you need to work on something technical, I don't know how you will do that."

Initially, I took this as information or advice. But as this started getting nowhere, I realised I was trying to resolve an issue while the onshore manager simply wanted to hold the reins of the team by stonewalling me–who was offshore, lesser cost to company, with relevant (AI/Data) experience to handle the engineering team. This is linked to onshore resources being insecure about their roles, as they belong to a higher cost centre (cost to company per employee is higher in the USA compared to India). Especially in technical project management roles, there is a strong possibility of being replaced by an offshore resource, as the company could save a good \$100,000 - \$150,000 per annum. This is one downside to the GCC model, the dynamics between onshore and offshore product/ project management getting a bit complicated.

I could understand his frustration as he was the sole breadwinner of his USA-based NRI family. But the systemic debunking of one's talent and potential makes you question: shouldn't mutual respect be enough to maintain a decent working relationship and function with trust? Why should someone climb the code Everest to be considered a "cool" leader especially in a non-technical role, as a lateral hire joining in a mid-senior position?

That's when you stop empathising and start being assertive.

Empathy has limits. Know when to call a spade a spade.

**Distract from Distraction**

Cut the chatter and forced small talk.

Have fewer people around. Choose your company.

Let your highest vibration resonate every day, even if for a few minutes.

Allow your most authentic thoughts to flow—the ones you had before the chaos took over.

People call it the "inner child." Personally, that sounds weird. I don't think I have a child inside me unless one of my eggs got fertilised.

I'm a fully functioning adult—with a dirty mind and pure intentions.

But yes, have **authentic conversations**, even if it upsets people.

Fewer friends, stronger boundaries. Quality over quantity.

Most Indians are terrified of being alone, which explains early marriages, constant socialising, and the obsession with "any love is better than no love."

Learn to separate categories:

- Clients are your stakeholders, their ability to give a shit about your well-being is closer to zilch, so don't demonise them, learn to understand their needs and build a deliverable based relationship. Detach yourself from their moods or volatility, for your own mental peace.
- Colleagues are people you are in constant competition with; to keep the competition healthy, have minimum expectations of human courtesies from your colleagues. It is a dog-eat-dog world out there.
- Work friends are great allies to blow off steam with a conversation, coffee, or cigarettes, not people who can be trusted with work related rants or genuine cries for help. That's what you have psychologists for.
- Classmates aren't lifelong soulmates; they are a bunch of 200 odd people who will remember you for your habits and tendencies at university, which might open doors or Pandora's boxes for you based on your approach.

We throw around words like *Anna* and *Akka* at work, devaluing real relationships—and, worse, dulling our intuition.

Resist the constant need to add emotional value to work-related equations. This helps keep things pragmatic and a matter of fact. Anyone running the same race as yourself can't approach you in a collaborative mindset, at best can be acquaintances at best. Any information you share about your personal life, financial problems, or future plans can and most probably be used against you.

This helps you stay authentic and channel your creativity rather than having a dopamine overload with half-baked versions of information and ideas from everywhere except your own mind. Authenticity is really our only competitive advantage as a race at this point!

**Art of Saying "No"**

Something I find lacking the most in cultures like ours is the art of saying "No". Often it is said later than it should be or in a fitful manner so that it is considered an emotional burst rather than a firm statement or reinforcement of boundaries.

Find the best, most authentic version of yourself.

If you haven't yet, start the journey–physically, mentally, emotionally, intellectually.

Anything that weighs down that light–be it a person, environment, or conversation–has to go.

Just like that school experiment with tuning forks, your authentic vibration will resonate only with the right surface.

Find your edge: be it communication, problem-solving, empathy, or discipline. Blend it with your skills and build your inner narrative.

Then let everything else be noise.

Personally, I leverage spiritual practices, even if they are religious in nature, to tune into that frequency. Whatever helps you connect, do that.

This practice makes you a **good** person, not necessarily a **nice** one.

Because the goal is not to be nice, quiet the contrary actually. To survive. To thrive.

AI seldom can say "No", because the parameters involved in tending to a non-favourable condition often require courage.

Courage to see the decisions through till their fruition. At the moment, AI hasn't been completely trained to make autonomous, emotionally valid decisions on behalf of humans. Which gives us hope that human intellect cannot be taken lightly.

The bottom line is that AI, like any other tech advancement needs attention, to be rationalised, leveraged, and propagated. You need to be able to apply yourself with it, the hype around it is also a form of gatekeeping.

# Chapter 12: The Ultimate Utopian Tech World

After all the stories, spirals, heartbreaks, betrayals, survival strategies, and karmic detours we've explored until now, it is time to stop obsessing about individual coping mechanisms and turn our lens toward the bigger demon—the system itself.

We've dissected the rot that employees face:

- the silent mental health epidemic,
- the battle between survival and dignity,
- and the inescapable corporate Chakravyuha in which millions of Indians are trapped.

But let's lift the veil now.

Let's look at the **macrocosm**, not just the **microcosm**.

Let's look at how India—a nation with **5.4 million people** working in technology—still functions as if it is trapped in a digital dystopia: rich in talent, poor in structure; wealthy in intellect, starving in systems; exporting brilliance, importing misery [2].

Because that is exactly what our **"Indian Dystopian Tech World"** has become: a civilisation with extraordinary potential, repeatedly sabotaged by archaic mindsets, weak infrastructure, outdated governance, exploitative corporate power, and an education system that still worships the UPSC syllabus more than innovation.

And even the gods would roll their eyes at this cosmic irony.

The law says 48 hours work week. India says, "...sure, but no."

In November 2025, the Indian government passed a law limiting IT employees to **8–10 hours per day, 48 hours per week.**

A historic milestone, right?

In theory: yes.

In reality: absolutely not.

Let's be honest.

No nation whose tech outsourcing economy runs on **T&M billing**, trans-continental client dependency, and hyper-competitive delivery cycles will ever be able to enforce such laws unless the ecosystem changes at every layer.

And forget the law for a second.

The problem is not about **how many** hours Indians work.

It's about **how meaningless, inefficient, poorly managed,** and **chaotically structured** those hours are.

If policymakers genuinely want to help India's massive tech workforce, they must first understand **how the system actually works inside the belly of the beast.** Because from the outside it looks like a glittering temple of opportunity, but inside it feels more like *Yamaloka* for anyone who is not protected by caste, region, gender, family wealth, or sheer luck.

**The Founders are Visionaries, the Middle Management are Gatekeepers.**

Let's give credit where due.

The founding teams of India's tech giants were visionaries.

Infosys, Wipro, TCS, HCL—these companies were built by purpose-driven leaders who believed in nation-building, not just profit.

These men/women had **vision**, **discipline**, **framework**, and **philosophy**.

They imagined an India that could outthink the world.

But as the founding philosophy trickles down the organisational pyramid, everything mutates.

By the time vision becomes execution, it loses its moral purity.

### The Delivery Bottleneck: Where Strategy Goes to Die

Let us assume a C-suite leader announces:

"We will file 100 intellectual property patents this year."

It falls on **middle managers,** the most undertrained, overpromoted, insecure layer of the organisation to:

- identify the domains for innovation
- select "critical resources"
- calculate weekly availability
- balance existing workload
- protect the team from burnout
- communicate with stakeholders
- redistribute work
- track progress
- and most importantly: **keep the humans alive long enough to innovate**

Guess what actually happens?

They dump IP work *on top of* existing workload...

...without removing anything.

...without providing backup.

...without coordinating with stakeholders.

So, the "critical resource" becomes the sacrificial goat.

And this is why **innovation in India suffocates:** not because Indians are not brilliant, but because they are **exhausted, overcommitted, and operating in survival mode**.

Even the gods cannot innovate under pressure.

*Ask Vishwakarma: he required cosmic peace to craft the universe. Yet when summoned urgently by the Pandavas to build Indraprastha, he created the palace amid chaos. In that haste, he introduced unnecessary complexities–magical pathways among them. One such illusion led Duryodhana to mistake a decorative pool for solid ground, humiliating him and ultimately triggering the Great Indian War.*

Likewise, innovation driven by pressure rather than clarity often produces massive, expensive blunders–manifesting today as data-security breaches, production failures, and systemic breakdowns.

**Process vs. People: The Indian Paradox**

India has world-class talent, but **terrible processes**.

Every company preaches Agile, Scrum, Kanban, OKRs.

Every new manager flaunts Jira like it is a magic wand.

But the reality?

**Nothing runs the way it was designed.**

Why?

Because most middle management transition from individual contributor roles without psychological, pedagogical, or communication training. Worse, many are promoted based on:

- regional favouritism
- longevity
- proximity to power
- obedience
- or sheer office politics
- not merit

So instead of building **process-oriented systems**, they build **person-dependent monopolies**:

- Knowledge Gatekeeping.
- One resource's absence delays the entire project.
- Critical information is not shared to safeguard positions. Transparency is seen as a threat.

This is the opposite of innovation.

This is feudalism dressed as corporate structure.

And India wonders why top talent chooses to migrate abroad or quit from burnout rather than thriving in their home ground.

### A Utopian Tech World: The Dream We Owe Ourselves

Here is the thesis:

**If India wants to retain its position as world's best delivery hub and outsourcing partner, it needs a centralised governing body that protects employees, standardises quality, enforces accountability, and ensures fairness.**

The Centralised Tech HR Council Should Include:

- Senior HR professionals trained in conflict resolution
- Labour lawyers
- Technology experts
- Women's welfare leaders
- Representatives from MNCs, startups, and mid-size firms
- Rotating elected employees (junior plus senior levels)

A modern Sabha. A digital Dharma Sabha.

Because right now, employees have nowhere to go except:

- Anonymous Reddit posts
- Glassdoor rants
- Blind confessions
- Passive-aggressive LinkedIn posts
- Group chats
- Therapy
- Or complete silence (and silence is costly)

HR department is a non-revenue-generating function, and its primary mandate is to protect the organisation. As a result, its priorities are closely aligned with senior leadership.

When a complaint threatens:

- senior management
- client relationships
- project timelines

- or the company's brand and reputation

HR is structurally inclined to choose the company—almost every time.

*Like Gandhari, who willingly blindfolded herself because her husband was blind by birth, HR can sometimes self-impose blindness in the name of duty and loyalty, making few choices outside leadership's purview. This is often framed as professionalism or neutrality, but it can limit meaningful intervention.*

This is why many organisations need a neutral, independent body, outside corporate politics, where employees can safely report:

- overwork
- mistreatment
- sexual harassment
- wage theft
- retaliation
- unfair labour practices

Without fear of being:

- blacklisted
- gaslit
- isolated
- demoted
- or quietly pushed out

Creating such systems isn't about undermining HR—it's about strengthening trust, accountability, and fairness across the organisation.

## Standardisation: The Backbone of Fairness

India desperately needs **industry-wide standardisation**:

**1. Standardised job roles**

Given the advancement of AI, the definitions of roles are blurring, with one person taking on the job of 3 people. So, standardising the job description across the industry helps reduce attrition based on overload or lack of clarity on the role.

**2. Standardised salaries**

±10% variance across companies.

No more pay disparity based on gender, age, or marital status. Helps increase employee loyalty, which is largely based on the better package offered by the next best company.

**3. Standardised benefits**

Provide better mental health care, paid leave with no obligation to attend meeting or respond to emails, and better company culture, so that people don't start quiet quitting.

**4. Standardised grievance channels**

Build and manage autonomous, semi-democratic HR bodies that help govern organisational HR departments especially in terms of grievances—to help eradicate toxic culture and enable better accountability.

**5. Standardised upskilling pathways**

To help employees stay on-par with the market's evolving requirements of skillset. This helps them utilise their skills for the benefit of the company they are currently employed at and be upskilled if they need to find a new job from layoffs.

Why?

Because without standardisation, India's tech economy becomes a jungle—where employees hop endlessly searching for dignity instead of spending time innovating.

## The Crisis of Indian Innovation

We need **to enable tech geniuses**—people who can think for society and build accordingly. When such talent partners with strong business thinking, that is the **sweet spot** where the greater good meets innovation and a sustainable paycheck.

We don't want to starve or burn out our talent. Encourage moonlighting; the goal is to create an ecosystem that offers **space, stability, and peace of mind**, allowing innovators to work on ideas that can realistically see the light of day when they go to the market.

We need collaboration across **all age groups**, bringing together diverse experiences, work ethic, wisdom, and agility. This diversity is essential if we are to build solutions for our local challenges—cleaner air, better roads, decentralised and skill-based education, and stronger policymaking.

We need policymakers who have lived the **ordinary lives of common people**, so they can truly understand and lead them.

Until then, we must ask ourselves: how can we claim to solve real-world problems for our country if we continue to function primarily as a **technology back office for others**—while other nations build with purpose, guided by goals like net zero commitments, GDP growth, and rising per capita income?

## The "Potayto–Potahto" Startups

With all due respect, most VC-funded startups in India today are replicas.

Same problem. Same model. Same deck.

Different logo.

30-minute deliveries.

Hyperlocal groceries.

Logistics apps.

Fintech apps.

Edtech apps.

A conveyor belt of monotony.

The mentally taxing part?

Many of these startups rely on:

- underpaid gig workers
- exploitation of the unorganised workforce
- high burn, low ethics
- predatory pricing
- unsustainable revenue models

Innovation is not solving the same problem 200 times.

It is creating **new** solutions for **new** problems.

Sridhar Vembu built Zoho by training **rural 12th-pass students** to code.

No IIT.

No IIM.

No fancy startup incubator.

No VC.

Just *vision* and *execution*.

That is the future India deserves. We have MSc holders serving 10-minute deliveries or driving cabs in urban India.

Are we truly generating employment, or are we exploiting cheap labour? There is no shame in any job. However, my point is about creating **meaningful employment**—where more people can enter the elite white-collar job market.

I believe there is enough success in this world for all of us to share. **One person's gain is not another person's loss**. That zero-sum thinking is a post-colonial hangover we need to unlearn. Together, we can—***as investors***—fund socio-economically empowering projects; ***as founders***—identify problems that solve more than just balance-sheet uptrends; and ***as an educated, aspiring workforce***—apply our knowledge instead of merely chasing ranks and marks.

We need more brilliant, audacious young people—being audacious for the **right reasons**.

The instant gratification economy of social media is numbing the fire that keeps one's authentic purpose alive. These tools should be working for us—not quietly draining our potential in the pursuit of short-lived dopamine spikes.

**Skill Gap: India's Broken Engine**

India's children spend 15–20 years mugging for exams.

- Regurgitating knowledge.
- Using GenAI to complete assignments.
- Buy fake thesis "projects."
- Competing for marks, not mastery.

In 2025, AI can write assignments faster than students can think.

So what is the point of this rote-learning circus?

Schools must teach:

- critical thinking
- design thinking
- collaboration
- apprenticeship
- problem solving
- early prototyping
- project-based learning
- financial literacy
- communication
- digital creation

Because by the time a student turns 21, they should know **what they are good at, how to apply it, and how to monetise it.**

Not just how to be obedient employees for MNCs.

There is immense potential in **skill-based education,** where children are empowered with Web 3.0 and Web 4.0 skills right from school, so they can enter the freelance market early. There are plenty of verified platforms where both rural and urban tech talent can sign up and work on live projects if they have the right technical and problem-solving skills. Why limit employment opportunities to only after graduation?

### A Future Worth Building

India's IT and BPO services contribute to 60% of its global services exported, which generated revenue close to 254.5 billion USD [21]. Roughly translates to the GDP of the country that first-ever invaded and tried to colonise India, Portugal [20].

We support Silicon Valley's digital ambitions. We built London's fintech backbone. We enable the Gulf's digital infrastructure.

We are still not claiming this as our soft power to engage workforce in humane manner.

If India wants to become global product-based tech leader—not just a world supplier of top-class IT talent—it must:

- protect its talent from migrating outside
- empower innovators and build humane workplaces
- focus on bridging skill gaps not just glorify education
- invest in employee well-being
- normalise rest and reward creativity
- create safe grievance systems
- involve tech experts in governance
- and cultivate leaders, not dictators

Because an unhappy workforce cannot innovate.

An overworked employee cannot dream.

A burnt-out mind cannot create.

A suppressed voice cannot lead.

A disrespected mind cannot think beyond survival.

And a system that silences its thinkers, doers, and radical minds will always be a cost-effective back-office to realise the dreams of money-alluring, capitalistic economies such as the USA, UK, and other countries.

# Final Thoughts

As you reach the end of this book, return to the very first exercise you did—the list of insecurities, fears, frustrations, and quiet wounds you brought into your work life. Read it again. Meet that earlier version of yourself with more kindness and clarity.

***"I, (your name), want to (build / become / overcome / evolve out of) ______***

***for (reason / purpose) ______***

***by (tentative deadline) ______."***

Now ask yourself:

Did those fears stay monsters—or did they turn into doorways?

Did you notice patterns you couldn't see before?

Did what scare you most also show you where your greatest growth lives?

***"If I can (change / release / interrupt / stop) ______,***

***then I will be able to (build / become / evolve into) ______***

***for (purpose) ______, by (timeline) ______."***

Now take that situation—or challenge—and use it as a stepping stone to your next level. Maybe it's a promotion you haven't asked for because imposter syndrome keeps you second-guessing yourself. Maybe it's a salary conversation you don't know how to navigate yet. Maybe it's a toxic work dynamic you want to change without getting emotionally overwhelmed.

Whatever it is, I hope this book helps normalise the struggle—and supports you in finding your own, unique solutions to your very real, very personal challenges.

This book was never about villainising the tech industry.

It was about humanising the people inside it.

This book is also a reminder.

If work stress has pulled your mental health into a dark place...

If you've carried work problems no one around you seems to understand...

If you're in debt, need support, yet tolerate unfair treatment because walking away feels impossible...

You are not alone.

There is community for what you're experiencing.

And there is a voice you can reclaim.

Things are changing—slowly, unevenly, but undeniably. A new generation of leaders is stepping up: less rigid, less discriminatory, more emotionally aware, and more open to inclusion and change. It's not perfect, but it's progress.

What you've read is a brutally honest look at corporate tech and office politics—for anyone entering the industry with rose-tinted glasses, or for those who still believe hard work alone guarantees fairness. It's not meant to discourage you, but to equip you.

India's tech ecosystem is rich in potential and deeply flawed in practice. Some problems demand individual courage. Others require systemic change—and that work cannot come only from the bottom. It must also come from boardrooms, founders, policymakers, and leaders shaping the future.

But the spark?

That can start with you.

My hope, as you close this book, is simple:

That you stop seeing yourself as a small cog in a massive system—and start recognising yourself as an active participant in India's digital story, one choice at a time.

*Like Arjuna heading back to the battlefield with clarity and renewed confidence after Krishna's Gita Upadesha (the most* GOAT-*ed pep talk of our lifetime).*

I hope this book empowers you to enhance the narrative about your reality.

Because for workplaces to become humane, for leadership to grow up, and for the tech world to truly mature—we need more people like you.

People who are whistle-blowers.

People who are troublemakers (for the right reasons of course!).

People who are trailblazers!

If even a few of you walk away feeling more confident in claiming your place—whether in this industry or elsewhere—then my purpose as a survivor has been served. As I shared in the prologue, by giving voice to my experiences and speaking the truths I once struggled to name, I hope to empower those who feel less supported or less heard, and in doing so, bring this cycle to a close for myself while helping others step out of the same matrix, one person at a time.

# Glossary

## 1. Organisation Structure

The arrangement of roles, responsibilities, and relationships within an organisation that determines how it operates. It defines reporting lines, hierarchies, and coordination mechanisms that help achieve business goals and enable communication across functions. Organisations may restructure based on mergers, acquisitions, growth, or revenue pressures.

**Figure 2:** Typical organisational structure in 2025, subject to change based on industry, size, and company goals (AI-generated, based on prompts from the author).

## 2. Project

A project is a temporary effort undertaken to create a unique product, service, or result, with a defined beginning, goal, timeline, and outcome.

### i. Onsite

Onsite refers to project work performed at the client's physical location. Team members collaborate directly with the client for requirement gathering, coordination, and real-time decision-making.

### ii. Offshore

Offshore refers to project work executed from a different country than the client's, typically to optimise costs and access global talent. Teams work remotely while following the client's timelines, processes, and delivery standards.

### iii. Onshore

Onshore refers to project work carried out within the same country as the client but at a different location. It combines local market understanding with remote or semi-remote execution.

### iv. Nearshore

Nearshore refers to project work carried out in a neighbouring or nearby country to the client. It offers cost advantages while maintaining closer time-zone alignment and cultural compatibility.

### 3. Team

A team is a group of individuals with complementary skills who work together toward a shared goal and are collectively responsible for outcomes.

### 4. Product Team

A cross-functional group responsible for deciding what to build, why to build it, and for whom. Product teams balance business objectives, user needs, and team capabilities.

### 5. Engineering Team

A group responsible for building, testing, deploying, and maintaining technology solutions. They translate ideas and designs into working systems—the muscle of the tech world.

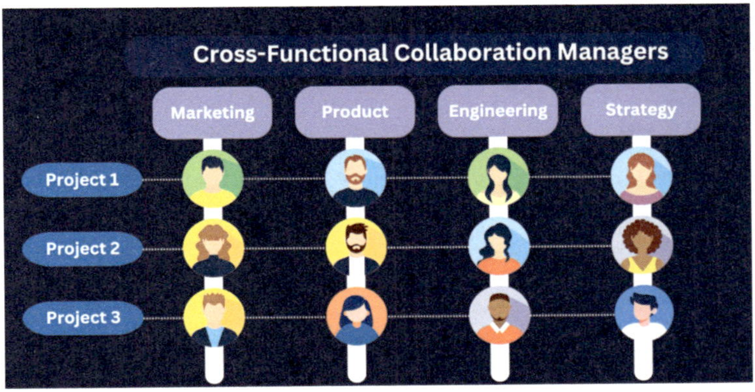


**Figure 3:** How various functions collaborate in modern tech organisations. Source: claap.io blog on cross-functional collaboration.

### 6. Jira

Jira is a digital task and project tracking tool used by teams to plan work, assign tasks, track progress, and manage workflows.

### 7. Stories, Tasks, Epics

Units of work used in tools like Jira.

Stories represent user-focused requirements.

Tasks are smaller actionable items.

Epics are large bodies of work broken down into multiple stories.

These are used in software, data, and AI projects to ensure traceability and accountability.

### 8. Agile Scrum

Scrum is an Agile framework where teams plan, build, review, and improve work in short, fixed cycles. It emphasises frequent feedback, adaptability, and incremental delivery.

### 9. Kanban

Kanban is a visual workflow management method that tracks work as it moves through stages such as "To Do," "In Progress," and "Done," with a focus on continuous delivery.

### 10. Sprint

A sprint is a short, fixed time period—usually one to two weeks—during which a team completes a defined set of planned work.

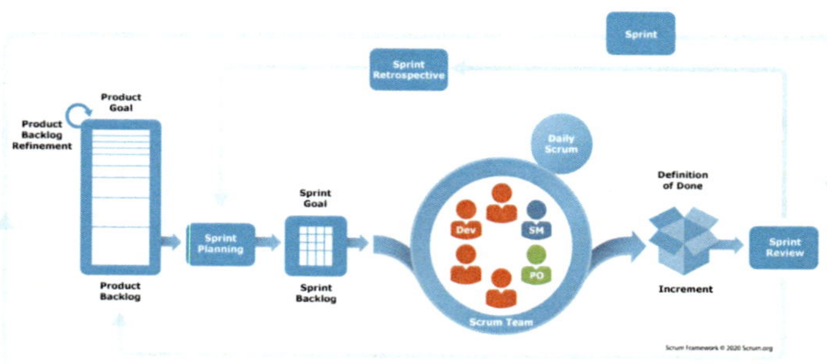


**Figure 4:** Roles and steps involved in one sprint. Scrum and Kanban are methodologies used to execute a sprint [19].

### 11. CTC (Cost to Company)

CTC is the total annual cost an employer incurs for an employee, including salary, benefits, bonuses, and statutory contributions. The take-home salary is what remains after deductions.

### 12. Service-Based Company [6]

A service-based company delivers work for clients, such as software development, IT services, or consulting. Revenue depends on people, time, and contractual engagements.

### 13. Product-Based Company [6]

A product-based company builds and sells its own products or platforms. Revenue is generated through product sales, subscriptions, or licensing.

### 14. Performance Improvement Plan (PIP)

A structured plan used by employers to address performance gaps by setting expectations, timelines, and measurable improvement goals.

### 15. ROI (Return on Investment)

ROI is a performance metric used to evaluate the efficiency or profitability of an investment relative to its cost.

### 16. KPI (Key Performance Indicator)

A KPI is a measurable value used to assess how effectively an individual, team, or organisation is achieving key objectives.

### 17. MVP (Minimum Viable Product)

An MVP is the simplest version of a product with just enough features to satisfy early users and gather feedback for future development.

### 18. Global Capability Centre (GCC)

A Global Capability Centre is an offshore or nearshore entity set up by multinational companies to build in-house capabilities across technology, operations, analytics, and shared services.

**19. Re-organisation**

Re-organisation refers to changes in a company's internal structure, roles, or reporting lines, often driven by strategic shifts, cost optimisation, or performance challenges.

**20. MNC (Multinational Corporation):**

A company that operates in multiple countries, with offices, production, or services spread across more than one nation.

**21. Web 3.0 Skills:**

Skills related to decentralised internet technologies, including blockchain, smart contracts, cryptocurrencies, decentralised applications (dApps), and digital asset management.

**22. Web 4.0 Skills:**

Skills associated with the intelligent and immersive web, where AI-driven systems, automation, IoT, and human-machine interaction work together to deliver personalised, predictive, and real-time digital experiences.

# References


1. https://www.mordorintelligence.com/industry-reports/india-software-services-export-industry-market
2. https://pib.gov.in/Pressreleaseshare.aspx?PRID=1847841&reg=3&lang=2
3. https://www.meity.gov.in/ministry/our-groups/details/software-industry-promotion-gN1EDOtQWa
4. https://www.ibef.org/industry/indian-it-and-ites-industry-analysis-presentation
5. https://www.gov.uk/guidance/visa-processing-times-applications-outside-the-uk
6. https://workat.tech/general/article/product-based-companies-vs-service-based-companies-dbzwhkqb2ieu#:~:text=Service%2DBased%20Companies%20are%20companies,your%20time%20and%20not%20impact
7. https://sageuniversity.in/blogs/highest-paying-jobs-india-salaries-skills-trends
8. https://www.reddit.com/r/IndiaStatistics/comments/1okl9dx/indias_economic_pyramid_2025_income_class/
9. https://www.business-standard.com/india-news/77-of-gen-z-students-shows-interest-in-technology-industry-report-124012200714_1.html
10. https://www.glassdoor.co.in/Salaries/entry-level-software-engineer-salary-SRCH_KO0,29.htm

11. https://www.moneycontrol.com/technology/it-firms-time-material-revenue-halves-to-35-over-20-years-as-clients-demand-accountability-innovation-article-12883750.html
12. https://www.thehindu.com/news/cities/bangalore/attrition-among-women-in-tech-sector-40-says-karnatakas-it-minister-priyank-kharge/article67016886.ece
13. https://spacelift.io/blog/women-in-tech-statistics
14. https://bestmediainfo.com/interviews/digital/only-5-women-reach-tech-leadership-roles-says-google-indias-preeti-lobana-9373768
15. https://www.indiatoday.in/lifestyle/relationship/story/india-ranks-2-for-office-romances-in-new-survey-2818208-2025-11-13
16. https://www.statista.com/statistics/320776/contribution-of-indian-it-industry-to-india-s-gdp/#:~:text=The%20industry%20has%20been%20generating,2024%20with%20estimate%20of%202025
17. Gartner – IT Services Definition: https://www.gartner.com/en/information-technology/glossary/it-services
18. https://doi.org/10.3345/cep.2021.00766
19. https://www.scrum.org/resources/what-is-a-sprint-in-scrum
20. https://cowrywise.com/blog/top-countries-in-the-world-by-gdp-per-capita/#:~:text=Table_title:%20Top%2050%20richest%20countries%20in%20the,Country:%20Lithuania%20%7C%20GDP:%2066%20billion%20%7C
21. https://www.ey.com/en_in/insights/india-at-100/how-india-is-emerging-as-the-world-s-technology-and-services-hub

22. https://www.drishtiias.com/daily-updates/daily-news-analysis/recognising-the-economic-value-of-unpaid-work-in-india#:~:text=Findings%20from%20the%20Valuation:%20The,equitable%20redistribution%20of%20caregiving%20responsibilities

# Special Mention

My sincere thanks to Advocate Shashwat Singh of Vox Populi Legal, Delhi, for his guidance and support as my legal advisor.

I also extend my gratitude to the staff of Third Wave, HSR Layout, Bengaluru, for providing a welcoming and author-friendly environment.

Finally, heartfelt thanks to Swati Gangadhar and Tanuja Reddy for playing a pivotal role during the editing process, especially at a time when my confidence was not at its best.

# About the Author

**Tushara Reddy** is an **AI Product Manager**, **founder**, and **author**, currently working full-time in a Bangalore-based multinational company where she builds and scales AI-driven products.

She earned her **MSc in Data Science with distinction** from **Queen Mary University of London** (Class of 2022). Before relocating to India, Tushara worked in **London** working as a **Data Product Manager**, leading data-led product initiatives in high-impact environments.

Tushara is also an exited **startup founder** who built **ReDesell (2020)**, a circular economy venture, supported by incubators and programmes including **Carbon13 (Cambridge)** and the **NSRCEL Women Startup Program, IIMBx**.

A debut author of an experiential memoir rooted in her lived journey through entrepreneurship, career transitions, leadership, and self-growth, Tushara is also a former **Toastmasters International leader and mentor**, and an accomplished public speaker known for her clarity, authenticity, and inspiration.

A fitness enthusiast and proud South Bangalorean, she shares her life with family, friends, and her 6-year-old indie she-dog, Missy.

Linkedin: linkedin.com/in/tushara-reddy-5a9733b8

